GREAT DANES BIBLE AND THE GREAT DANE

Your Perfect Great Dane Guide

Covers Great Danes, Great Dane Puppies, Great Dane Training, Great Dane Size, Great Dane Nutrition, Great Dane Health, History, & More!

By Mark Manfield

© DYM Worldwide Publishers, 2018.

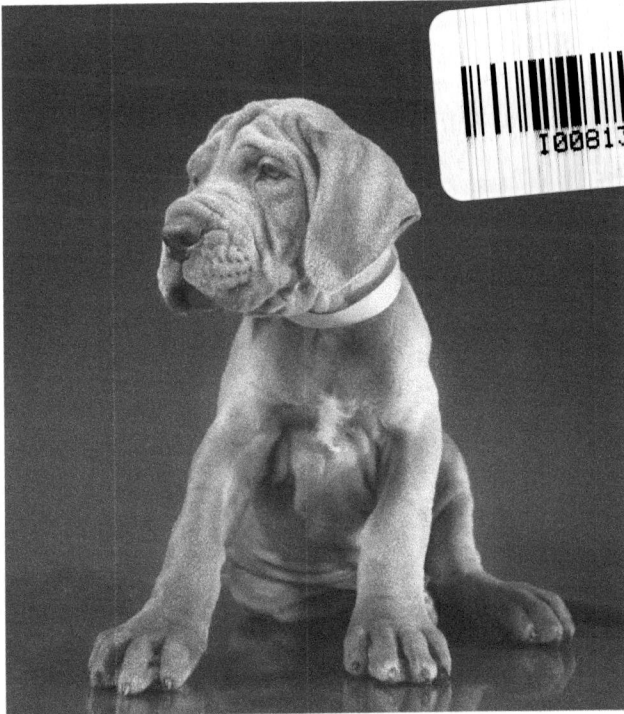

Published by DYM Worldwide Publishers 2018.

ISBN: 978-1-911355-64-9

Copyright © DYM Worldwide Publishers, 2018
2 Lansdowne Row, Number 240 London W1J 6HL

Disclaimer and Legal Notice. This product is not legal or medical advice and should not be interpreted in that manner. You need to do your own due diligence to determine if the content of this product is right for you. The author, publisher, distributors, and or/affiliates of this product are not liable for any damages or losses associated with the content in this product. While every attempt has been made to verify the information shared in this publication, neither the author, publisher, distributors, and/or affiliates assume any responsibility for errors, omissions, or contrary interpretation of the subject matter herein. Any perceived slights to any specific person(s) or organization(s) are purely unintentional. We have no control over the nature, content, and availability of the websites listed in this book. The inclusion of any website links does not necessarily imply a recommendation or endorse the views expressed within them. DYM Worldwide Publishers takes no responsibility for, and will not be liable for, the websites being temporarily or being removed from the Internet. The accuracy and completeness of the information provided herein, and opinions stated herein are not guaranteed or warranted to produce any particular results, and the advice or strategies, contained herein may not be suitable for every individual. The author, publisher, distributors, and/or affiliates shall not be liable for any loss incurred as a consequence of the use and application, directly or indirectly of any information presented in this work. This publication is designed to provide information regarding the subject matter covered. The information included in this book has been compiled to give an overview of the topics covered. The information contained in this book has been compiled to provide an overview of the subject. It is not intended as medical advice and should not be construed as such. For a firm diagnosis of any medical conditions, you should consult a doctor or veterinarian (as related to animal health). The writer, publisher, distributors, and/or affiliates of this work are not responsible for any damages or negative consequences following any of the treatments or methods highlighted in this book. Website links are for informational purposes only and should not be seen as a personal endorsement; the same applies to any products or services mentioned in this work. The reader should also be aware that although the web links included were correct at the time of writing they may become out of date in the future. Any pricing or currency exchange rate information was accurate at the time of writing but may become out of date in the future. The Author, Publisher, distributors, and/or affiliates assume no responsibility for pricing and currency exchange rates mentioned within this work.

Table of Contents

Introduction

G iant, tall, and massive ... the Great Dane usually comes first to mind, when you think of a dog with these characteristics. They are one of the tallest and largest dog breeds in the world, and they always have a place in this category of world records. It is known as the "Apollo of Dogs" because of its sturdy but elegant stature. Despite its intimidating size, these dogs are calm and have a mild temperament. In fact, they are fondly known as gentle giants.

Giant, tall, and massive ... the Great Dane usually comes first to mind when you think of a dog with these characteristics.

13

The American Kennel Club describes the Great Dane as having a combination of a "regal, dignified, strong, and elegant appearance. Its body is well-formed, smooth, and muscled. It doesn't appear clumsy when it walks; the Great Dane's gait is graceful, thanks to its proportionately long legs. Its neck is long and graceful, and on top of it is a massive head, which is long and narrow." Their paws are massive and as big as a man's hand!

The Great Dane has been popularly known as a house companion, but you would be surprised to find out that it was originally bred to be a hunting and working dog. Many historical murals, as early as the 13th century, depict large boarhounds that look similar to the Great Dane. Around the 16th to the 17th century, they became companions to their noble owners who hunted bear, boar, and deer.

It is a great family dog and is gentle and playful with children. Its hunting instincts have been bred out through generations, and they rarely show aggressive behavior. It is essential, however, to socialize the Great Dane while it is still young. Doing this early on will train it not to react to strangers and to new environments negatively. Even though it has a peaceful demeanor, it will not hesitate to keep its guard up and defend its pack.

Despite its large build, the Great Dane is susceptible to a lot of health conditions. Surprisingly, they are one of the dog breeds that have the shortest lifespan. The average lifespan of the Great Dane is only 7 years, while other dogs can live up to 15 years. Among the health conditions, you need to watch out for are wobbler syndrome and bloat, which can be fatal for your Great Dane if not attended to immediately.

Because of its size, you need to provide it with ample space to move around. This dog is not ideal for small living spaces, such as apartments, where it does not have much room to stretch out its legs. You may find yourself picking over things that have fallen because your Great Dane keeps on knocking them over with its tail.

The Great Dane is statuesque and is considered as a luxury dog breed. Indeed, this dog never fails to inspire awe from anyone who is fortunate enough to see one!

CHAPTER 1

History of The Great Dane

Illustrations depicting dogs that look similar to the Great Dane already appeared as early as 3000 B.C. These figures were found in various locations, such as in Egypt and Greece. During ancient times, these dogs were known as boarhounds and were the favored companions of hunters because of their size, agility, and strength.

The Great Dane has been popularly known as a house companion, but you would be surprised to find out that it was originally bred to be a hunting and working dog.

Despite the word "Dane" in its name, the Great Dane did not hail from Denmark. In fact, this dog breed largely proliferated in Germany and Austria and was called *Englischer Hund*. Its origins can be traced back to the cross-breeding of the English Mastiff and Irish Wolfhounds. They were regarded as luxury dogs and even shared sleeping quarters with their owners, who were nobles and royalty.

What is the History and Background of The Great Dane?

No information states the exact age of the Great Dane. However, they have been around for thousands of years. Illustrations of dogs that are similar to the Great Dane were seen in Egyptian monuments dating back to 3000 B.C. In the 14th to 13th centuries B.C., canines that resemble the Great Dane were already depicted in frescoes in ancient Greece, specifically in Tiryns. These dogs were known as boarhounds and were seen centuries up to the Hellenistic era. From the 5th century A.D., many runestones and coins from Scandinavia and Denmark illustrated larger dogs. Old Norse poems, mainly known in English as the Poetic Edda, also mentioned these boarhounds. At least seven skeletons of giant dogs that date back to the 5th century B.C. to the 1st century A.D. are in possession of the University of Copenhagen Zoological Museum. These dogs were also described in ancient Chinese literature in 1121 B.C.

Boarhounds in these ancient times have a drastic difference with the Great Danes of today. These dogs from thousands of years past were shorter, heavier, stockier, and more muscular. They looked more similar to the Mastiff than the Great Dane.

In Austria and Germany, the stature of boarhounds was improved with the Molossian hound, Suliot dog, and some particular imports from Greece. By the middle of the 16th century, nobles from many European countries started to import muscular and long-legged dogs from England. These dogs' origins were from crossbreeds between the English Mastiffs and Irish Wolfhounds. As these dogs' population increased, they were called as *Englische Docke* or *Englische Tocke*.

In Germany, they were known as *Englischer Hund*. It has been documented that in 1592, the Duke of Braunschweig assembled a pack of 600 male Great Danes during a boar hunt. In the middle of the 16th to the 17th century, these dogs were bred in significant numbers, and the German noblemen took the largest and fiercest dogs to guard their estate. The German nobles admired these dogs so much; they began to take the best specimens as guard dogs. These top dogs became the companions of the wealthy aristocrats and lived with them in their large estates. The royalty's favorite dogs slept with them in their bedchambers. These dogs were known as *Kammerhunde* (chamber dogs) and were used to protect sleeping princes from assassination attempts. They wore gilded collars lined with velvet and enjoyed the luxurious life their owners lived.

During the 19th century, this breed was called the "German boarhound" in English-speaking countries. The Germans desired to market the dog as a luxury breed, and not as a working dog. Because of this, they tried to introduce names such as "German Dogge" and "German Mastiff." Due to the rising tensions between Germany and its neighboring counties, the dog was referred to as the "Great Dane." This name originated from the *grand danois* in Georges-Louis Leclerc, Comte de Buffon's *Histoire Naturelle, générale et particulière* in 1755.

In 1876, the Great Dane was declared as the national dog of Germany. Owners and enthusiasts of the breed enforced that the dog will be called the *Deutsche Dogge*, and other names that were used abolished. The Deutsche Dogge Club of Germany was formed in 1891 and described the official standard of the breed.

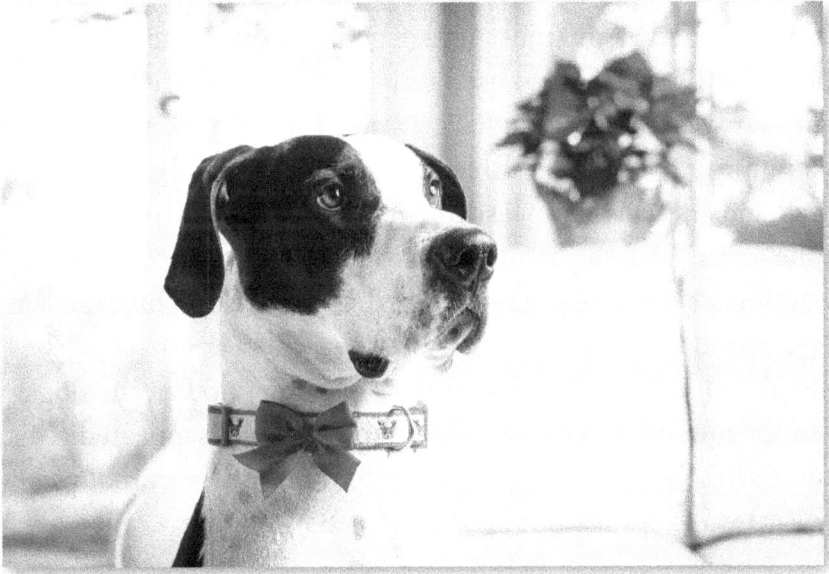

In 1876, the Great Dane was declared as the national dog of Germany.

The Great Dane started to come to the United States in the middle of the 1800s. The American Kennel Club officially recognized the breed in 1887. The German Mastiff Club of America was established in 1889 to gather owners of this breed. The group's name was changed to the Great Dane Club of America two years later.

Modern-day Great Danes rarely live the lifestyle of their boarhound ancestors. The breed has been selectively bred to be docile, conforming, and having a mild temperament. They are popularly known to be affectionate companions and great family pets.

What Were Great Danes Bred For?

The Great Dane was initially developed in England and Germany and bred to hunt European wild boar. This animal was considered as the most savage game at that time in Europe. The Great Dane was also used to hunt bears and deer at royal courts. It was necessary to have a strong, intelligent, and agile dog as a hunting companion. Breeders combined the Greyhound's speed and the English Mastiff's muscle strength. This resulted in the Great Dane's personality and characteristics to be suited to perform such a task. They worked as catch dogs, holding the target game in place until their hunter owners approached the animal and killed it. When firearms became popular, the dogs used for the old techniques of hunting slowly disappeared. This caused the *Englische Dogge* to become rare, and from that point forward was kept for hobby and luxury.

The owners saw the Great Dane suffering from shredded ears due to the razor-sharp tusks of the wild boar. To prevent this, they cropped the dogs' ears short and pointy. When the dog's purpose for hunting declined, ear cropping became a controversial practice and was ultimately banned in Europe.

Great Dane Dogs In Popular Culture

Perhaps the most famous Great Dane character in pop culture is Hanna-Barbera's *Scooby-Doo*. The cartoon show started in 1969, and since then has spawned many franchises which continue today.

Another Hanna-Barbera cartoon character who is also a Great Dane is Astro from *The Jetsons*. Astro is portrayed as a clumsy and dim-witted dog but is very loyal to his family.

Marmaduke was a newspaper comic strip created by Brad Anderson from 1954 to 2015. It featured the eponymous Great Dane and revolved around the Winslow family and their lives. In 2010, a movie version of the same name was produced, with Owen Wilson as the voice actor for Marmaduke.

Another Great Dane movie star was Brutus in Walt Disney's *The Ugly Dachshund* (1966). The plot involves the Garrison family adopting a Great Dane when he was rejected by his mother. They named him Brutus and allowed their Dachshund, who just gave birth to her own litter of puppies, to wean him. Growing up with his Dachshund sisters, Brutus thinks he is one of them and acts more like a Dachshund than a Great Dane.

Other famous Great Danes: Alexander Pope, an English poet (1688-1744) owned a Great Dane whom he named Bounce. Pope never left his house without Bounce by his side. Since the poet was crippled, physically weak, and received frequent threats caused by his lampoons, he needed Bounce for protection. Bounce had a permanent place in the poet's pages when the latter created the satirical poem "Bounce to Fop." Bounce was also illustrated along with Pope in the painting "Alexander Pope and His Dog, Bounce" (1718) by Jonathan Richardson.

Just Nuisance is a male Great Dane and the only dog to be officially enlisted in the Royal Navy. Just Nuisance's role was mainly a morale booster during World War II. A statue of Just Nuisance was erected in Simon's Town to commemorate his life. Full military honors were displayed when Just Nuisance was buried.

Great Dane Records – World's Largest and Tallest Great Dane

When it comes to world records of the largest and tallest dogs, Great Danes always have a spot.

Giant George (USA) held the title of tallest dog in The Guinness Book of World Records from 2010 to 2012. He measured at 41 in. (104 cm.) at the shoulder, and stands at 7 ft. 3 in. (2.21 m.) when standing on his hind legs. George weighed 245 lb. (111 kg.), which is 100 lb. (45 kg.) heavier than the average Great Dane. David Nasser bought and owned George when he was still a 7-week-old pup. George lived for eight years before he died on October 17, 2013.

In 2012 and 2013, the Guinness Book of World Records proclaimed a male Great Dane named 'Zeus' as the world's tallest dog, taking over Giant George's record. When standing on his hind legs, Zeus measured a towering 7 ft. and 5 in. (2.26 m.). He is two inches taller than Giant George. He is owned by Kevin and Denise Doorlag from Otsego, Michigan (USA). Doorlag reported Zeus to have died from natural causes and old age. The dog lived for 5 years, from 2008 to 2014.

Freddy the Great Dane (UK) snagged the title of "World's Tallest Living Dog – Male" on December 19, 2016. Guinness World Records awarded Freddy the title with his measurement that exceeded his predecessors, Zeus and Giant George. Freddy measures at 40.75 in. (1.03 m.), towers at 7 ft. 6 in. (2.3 m.) when standing on his hind legs, and weighs 200 lb. (90.72 kg.). He was born in 2012 and lives in Leigh-on-Sea with his owner Claire Stoneman, and his sister Fleur.

European Great Dane and American Great Dane – What's the Difference?

The European Great Dane tends to be bigger and broader than the American Great Dane. The European Great Dane's average weight is 180 lb. (81.65 kg.). It can weigh more, between 220 to 240 lb. (99.8 to 108.86 kg.). It shows more of the Mastiff characteristics, which means it has a blockier body and a heavier head.

On the other hand, the American Great Dane's weight ranges from 125 to 135 lb. (56.7 to 61.24 kg.). It shows more of the Greyhound qualities; it looks sleeker, thinner, and more graceful. The American Great Dane also grows faster; it matures when they are two years old while the European Great Dane grows until it is five years old.

CHAPTER 2

What Do You Need to Know About the Great Dane? Great Danes 101

L earn more about the Great Dane's anatomy and what makes it a regal breed. The American Kennel Club (AKC) provides standards on how a Great Dane should appear. This chapter also discusses the different beautiful coats that Great Danes can sport. Discover if this breed can adapt to different lifestyles, and what you need to do to develop your Great Dane.

*Great Danes are known as gentle giants and
have a temperate personality.*

Is the Great Dane the best pet for you? This chapter will also provide information on what the dog's needs are and how your family can live with one. Also, find out how your kids and other pets can live with a gigantic family member.

Great Danes As Pets – Who Are They Suited For?

Great Danes are known as gentle giants and have a temperate personality. They are moderately playful, which makes them great with children. An aspiring Great Dane owner must be willing to provide ample space and other needs that the dog demands. The owner must be prepared to appropriate a substantial budget to pay for the Great Dane's needs.

The Great Dane is the perfect dog if you are looking for one that ...

- Is huge, but has an elegant build.
- Has a smooth and shiny coat that can be easily maintained.
- Is easy-going and has a mild temperament and is usually non-aggressive.
- Requires moderate exercise.
- Has an intimidating stature that works as an effective deterrent.

The Great Dane may not be the best dog for you if...

- You are not prepared to repair any home damages caused by the dog.
- You are not fond of excessive slobbering and drooling.
- You are not prepared to care for the Great Dane's health issues.
- You do not want to handle potential legal liabilities, such as public perception, future bans on the breed, insurance issues, and possibilities of a lawsuit.

Purebred Great Dane Standards

The American Kennel Club (AKC) describes the Great Dane as regal in its appearance, where it combines dignity, strength, and elegance with its great size. It has a powerful, well-formed, and smoothly muscled body. It is considered as one of the giant working breeds. It is unique in its general conformation, in that it must be so well balanced that it never appears clumsy. The Great Dane should also move with a long reach and powerful drive.

Great Dane Dog General Appearance

The Great Dane has a sleek and athletic build with a muscular body. The size of its head is huge and is long and narrow. Its neck is long and graceful in appearance and is set high. Its body is proportional to its length and height. Its front legs stand perfectly straight and end in round paws with dark toenails. Its tail is thick which gradually thins out to a point at the end. The Great Dane's muzzle comes in black, blue/black, or spotted black. Its eyes are medium-sized and are deep and dark. A female Great Dane may have a body that is longer than her height.

The Great Dane has a sleek and athletic build, with a muscular body.

What Does a Full Grown Great Dane Look Like?

A fully grown adult male Great Dane can measure 32 in. (81.28 cm.) from its withers. A female Great Dane can stand at 30 in. (76.2 cm.), when measured from its withers. Great Danes have naturally floppy ears and a massive head that is narrow and flat on top. Its body is long, muscular, and the front legs are straight. It has a medium-length tail, that is thick at the base and thins down below the hocks.

Great Dane Full Size – How Large Can They Get?

A full-sized Great Dane can grow to over 40 in. (101 cm.) from the withers, and towers at 7 ft. (2 m.) tall when it stands on its hind legs!

Great Dane Average Weight – How Heavy Do They Get?

A Great Dane's average weight is around 100-120 lb. (45-54 kg.). More massive Great Danes can weigh even more, up to around 150-200 lb. (63-90 kg.)!

Are Great Danes Rare?

Great Danes have been around since the 1600s and have become beloved companions to many families over the centuries. However, to answer the question "are Great Danes rare?" we would have to turn our attention to their coat colors.

Six coat colors adhere and are accepted as Great Dane breed standards. These are black, blue, harlequin, mantle, fawn, and brindle. Great Danes that are outside of this color family should not be thought of as "rare," but as incorrect color conformation. Unscrupulous and dishonest breeders would sometimes market these dogs as "unique," "rare," or "exotic," and will put a hefty price tag on them. Breeding to a color standard may not necessarily equate to a healthier dog, but you can be confident that the breeder was at least obeying the color code of ethics for Great Danes.

Great Dane Tails

The Great Dane's tail is positioned high but is not entirely leveled with the top line. It is broad at the base and gently thins toward the end. It should hang straight when the dog is at rest. It should curve slightly when it moves around, but it should never bend above the level of its back.

This dog breed is notoriously known for its "happy tail syndrome." Also known as "splitting tail" and "kennel tail," the happy tail syndrome is when a dog wags its tail so hard it hits walls and objects with much force. This can cause the tail to break open, get injured, or lacerated. Wounds caused by the happy tail syndrome must be treated immediately, to avoid infections.

Great Dane Ears

The ears are positioned high and are medium in size. It can appear in its natural floppy form, where it folds forward, the top line levels with the skull, and hangs near the cheeks. Owners can choose to have the ears cropped, which must stand straight in appearance.

Great Dane Cropped Ears

Ear cropping in dogs involves removing part or all of the pinnae or auricles, which is the externally visible flap of the animal's ears. The process is usually done on puppies at 7 to 12 weeks of age. It is performed in a cropping operation, which afterward, the wound edges are closed with stitches. It also sometimes entails taping the ears, to make them appear pointy.

Great Dane ear cropping was widely practiced when the dogs were used to hunt European wild boars. These vicious animals were dangerous to hunt. Many dogs received lethal ear injuries when they were bitten, cut, or torn by the boar's sharp teeth and tusks. Owners perceived that short pointy ears would decrease the impact of the boar's blows on the dogs. Since then, ear cropping was widely practiced. Today some owners prefer their Great Dane's ears cropped only for aesthetic value, and this does not serve any practical function, beyond aesthetics.

Great Dane Coats

According to the AKC standard, the Great Dane's coat shall be short, thick, and clean with a smooth and shiny appearance.

Different Great Dane Colors

There are five solid colors that a Great Dane can have. However, there are only three solid colors that are accepted as breed standards: black, blue, and fawn. As per AKC criteria, any Great Dane that does not fall within the color classifications, must be disqualified in dog shows.

Below are the Great Dane solid coat colors that are accepted by AKC standards:

- **Great Dane Black.** A black Great Dane should have a glossy coat. Ideally, the dog should have a solid black coat all throughout its body. A white marking that appears on the dog's chest is a common appearance, but is not desirable.

- **Black Great Dane Puppies.** Pure black Great Dane puppies can be produced by breeding dogs who have a solid black coat, or if one of the parents have the "blue" gene. Puppies who have a white mark on their chest may be an offspring of a harlequin-harlequin or harlequin-black breeding pair.

- **Great Dane Blue.** The AKC standard for the blue Great Dane is that it should have a steel blue coat. Any other variety or markings on its coat are not desirable and will be faulted to the extent of deviation. Blue Great Danes with blue eyes are not an uncommon instance, but be wary of breeders who sell "rare, blue-eyed and blue-coated" Great Danes. Other eye colors can be amber, dark brown, or light brown.

- **Great Dane Blue Puppies.** Blue Great Dane puppies are produced when both parents have the recessive "blue" gene. A blue Great Dane puppy can be an offspring from a black-black or blue-black breeding pair.

- **Fawn Great Danes.** The fawn color is the most popular Great Dane coat and one that is easily recognized. It is characterized in a shade that ranges from very light tan, yellow, dark tan, or gold. It is also common for fawn Great Danes to have a black mark, or mask, on their face. When a fawn Great Dane lacks this dark color pigment, such a case is referred to as "dilute." This is caused by cross-color breeding, in the litter's lineage.

According to the AKC standards, fawn Great Danes should have a yellow gold body coat and a black mask. The black markings should appear on the rims of the eyes and on the eyebrows, and may also show on the dog's ears and tail tip. It is considered undesirable if the dog has other varieties of color or marking on its chest and toes.

- **Fawn Great Dane Puppies.** A Great Dane puppy with a dark pigment on its face, or mask, is produced when one of its parents carry the "mask" gene.

Other Great Dane Solid Coat Colors

White Great Danes

A solid white coat is the most unusual color for a Great Dane. It is also a sign that the dog is vulnerable to genetic abnormalities.

White Great Dane Puppies

White Great Dane puppies are commonly produced from a merle or harlequin breeding pair. The merle genes limit the melanocytes' function of producing pigments. This may also cause deafness and eye problems for puppies that acquire these genes.

Brown Great Danes

This coat color is also often referred to as "red." This color is sometimes mistaken to be blue or even cream. You only need to look at its color to discern if it is a brown Great Dane. A dilute Great Dane will have a rosy-brown nose with a slight grayish tint. Blue Great Danes have a gray, dark gray, or black nose.

Brown Great Dane Puppies

Great Dane puppies of this color are produced when one or both of their parents have the brown or chocolate recessive gene.

Different Great Dane Coats with Markings

There are only three coat markings that are recognized by the AKC. These are mantle, harlequin, and brindle. Any difference in color or markings from each of the coat's characteristics shall be faulted to the extent of the deviation, which is a cause for disqualification in dog show competitions.

Mantle Great Danes

The mantle color markings look identical to the Boston Terrier. This caused mantle Great Danes to be referred to as "Bostons" until the late 1990s. Mantles are strictly black and white, and must not have any merle (grey) patches on their coat. Any other markings or patches will make them considered as a heavily marked or blanketed harlequin.

The AKC's standards for the mantle Great Dane are as follows:

- The color should be black and white with a solid black blanket extending over its body.
- The head is black, and the muzzle is white; white blaze is optional.
- A whole white collar is preferred.
- Its chest should have a white patch.
- White marks appear on part or whole on fore and hind legs.

- The tail is black with a white tip.
- Small white markings and a break in the white collar is acceptable.

Mantle Great Dane Puppies

Mantle Great Dane puppies are born from one or both parents that are harlequins, merles, and/or mismarked blacks.

Harlequin Great Danes

The AKC standard for this coat pattern are as follow:

- The base color shall be pure white with black-torn patches that are irregularly well-distributed over the entire body.
- The black patch should never be big enough for it to appear like a blanket, nor too tiny that it looks like stripes or ripples.
- A few small grey spots may be acceptable, but not desirable.
- A white base with single black hairs appearing through, which gives a salt and pepper impression, may also be eligible, but not preferable.

It is interesting to note that no two harlequin coat patterns are the same. You will never know how a harlequin Great Dane will truly look at maturity, until it is full-grown.

Don't be alarmed if your harlequin Great Dane has different eye colors, as this is not an uncommon occurrence. One eye may be blue, while the other one may be brown or dark.

Harlequin Great Dane Puppies

Most people who are not experts on dogs or unfamiliar with the breed often mistake a growing harlequin Great Dane puppy as a Dalmatian. To produce these beautifully patched harlequin Great Dane puppies, it's not as simple as breeding two full harlequin Great Danes. One of the parents may carry genes of different colors, such as black, blue, and merle. It requires extensive breeding experience, many litters, and mismarks before a successful harlequin breeder finds the perfect breeding combination. A newborn harlequin Great Dane puppy's nose will appear pink at first, but as it matures, the color will typically darken to black or a darker pink with spots.

Brindle Great Danes

A brindle Great Dane's coat will appear as a pattern of stripes: red and black, fawn and black, or charcoal and grey. Light fawn, golden brown, deep golden red, or a pale color with a black tint can be the base color of a brindle Great Dane's coat.

AKC standards for brindle Great Danes are as follows:

- The coat's base color is yellow gold, and always brindled with strong black cross stripes in a chevron pattern.
- A black mask is preferred. Black should show on the eye rims and eyebrows, and may also be visible on the ears and tail tip.
- A more preferred coat is a color that is more intense, and the brindling more distinct and even.
- Too much or too little brindling, are equally undesirable.

- It is also undesirable if the dog's coat has white markings on its chest and toes.
- Dirty colored brindles are also not desirable.

Brindle Great Dane Puppies

Brindle puppies can be born from a breeding pair that consists of two brindles. Fawn puppies can also be produced from such a pair. If your Great Dane has perfect color conformation, it does not guarantee that the pups will inherit the same color. The puppies will be born with a brindle coat, but the color and shade of their fur can vary. Brindle puppies are also healthier in general than harlequin puppies. There are fewer genetic health issues that they are likely to acquire, such as vision and hearing problems, that are common in harlequin litters.

Other Great Dane coats with markings that are not recognized by the AKC:

Merle Great Danes

A Great Dane with a merle coat appears similar to the harlequin. The difference between the two is the base coat color. Merles can have a range of color base coats with dark spots. The coat pattern can be a combination of the harlequin and the mantle.

A Great Dane with a merle coat.

Be careful of breeders who market merle Great Danes as "rare" and demand a higher price for the dog.

Some of the "rare" colors that they may claim, include:

- **Fawn merle.** The coat is fawn, light cream to tan, with dark spots and speckles.

- **Chocolate merle.** Coat's spots appear more reddish in color.

- Brindle merle: stripes blend in and out of the base coat. Stripes can also appear to be broken or spotted.

- **Mantle merle.** The base coat is white and has a mantle pattern. The mantle appears silver, light to dark grey. The pattern is also spotted or speckled.

- **Blue merle.** The coat is dark blue or brownish blue and has dark spots. Pigmentation of the nose and skin can also appear bluish-black.

- **Silver or platinum merle.** The base coat is light silver or grey. It is also spotted or speckled, which is dark in color. The nose is typically black.

- **Tri-colored merle.** The coat can be a combination of several colors, but three distinct shades appear prominent.

Merle Great Dane Puppies

Merle Great Danes puppies can come from harlequin litters. Merle breeding is perceived as unethical color crossbreeding by the Great Dane Club of America. Merles are also very vulnerable to sickly puppies that are predisposed to health issues. If the "merle" gene exists in both parents, it can produce puppies that are stillborn, deaf, blind, or genetically abnormal.

What Is the Great Dane Temperament?

Based on AKC official standards, a Great Dane "must be spirited, courageous, never timid; always friendly and dependable. This physical and mental combination is the characteristic which gives the Great Dane the majesty possessed by no other breed."

Great Dane puppies must be socialized more frequently than most other breeds, to develop their confidence and build their stable temperament.

What Do You Need to Know About Great Dane Behavior?

Great Danes have a mild and affectionate personality. They are also moderately playful, which makes them gentle and good with children. They can live with other animals, especially if they were raised with them.

They will not hesitate to defend their homes, and their colossal size will often intimidate anyone who tries to break in. They tend to be aggressive towards other dogs they are not familiar with, so it is imperative to socialize them.

Great Danes are intelligent and easy to train, but they can become stubborn if you have not asserted your dominance, early on. They can become hard-headed learners, so obedience training is vital. They are sensitive and respond more to positive reinforcement, than negative. Harsh verbal and non-verbal cues confuse them and make them distrustful.

Great Dane Life Expectancy – How Long will the Great Dane Live with You?

This dog breed has one of the shortest lifespans of any breed. On average they live 6 to 8 years.

Great Dane Guard Dog – Is This the Right Breed for The Job?

"Its bark is worse than its bite." This statement is true for Great Danes. It produces a loud bark due to its large size. Its bark should be enough to deter intruders or give a clear warning of the threat.

Despite its famous image of a being "gentle giant," one should never underestimate a Great Dane on guard. Its bite may not be lethal enough to cause injuries, but its muscular body and size are strong enough to tackle trespassers.

It may require some training to develop your Great Dane to become an effective guard dog. As the aggressiveness of this dog has been bred out over the years, it has developed a gentler personality.

Great Dane Show Dogs – How Can You Maintain Them?

To nurture a Great Dane for show dog competitions, it will need several things. Proper nutrition and diet are essential. You also need to ensure that clean and fresh water is available at all times. Proper exercise is also vital to maintain its weight and keep it healthy. Consult with your veterinarian and/or breeder to discover the best food, the frequency of meals, and the exercise routine suitable for your Great Dane.

To take care of its external appearance, its nails should regularly be trimmed with a nail clipper or grinder. This will prevent overgrowth, splitting, and cracking. To avoid infections in its ears, frequently check and clean it when you see a build-up of wax or debris. Brush its teeth routinely to stop the formation of cavities, bad breath, tooth decay, and gum disease.

Great Dane Hunting – Can This Breed Be Your Hunting Companion?

Centuries ago, hunters used boarhounds (ancestors of the Great Danes) to accompany them when pursuing and killing wild boars. They needed dogs who were powerful and bold.

As hunting ceased to be widely practiced, these dogs evolved from being ferocious hunters to fabulous show dogs. The belligerence has been bred out of these canines, and now modern-day Danes enjoy a more leisurely lifestyle. They have become more docile and excellent additions to families. So, if you're looking for a dog to be your hunting sidekick, you may want to pass on the Great Dane.

Is the Great Dane The Best Dog for Your Family?

You need to assess your family's lifestyle before even considering a Great Dane. Your family must be willing to cater to the dog's enormous size. The Great Dane will require large quantities of food, which will also equate to allocating a bigger budget. Your family must also be willing and capable of taking it out for exercise. Someone must also be dedicated to training it, or else your Great Dane will become unruly and will wreck your home.

Do the Great Dane And Children Get Along?

Great Danes can form strong bonds with children, especially if they grow up together when they are young. Their gentle personality can be an excellent fit for your kids. Socialize and train your Great Dane early on, to develop their temperament in a positive way.

However, you must keep in mind to monitor any interaction between your children and the dog. Your Great Dane can become too excited and unintentionally knock your child down, or whip it with its 24-inch happy tail, causing injury.

Until a Great Dane has adapted to living with a small child, never let your kids play rough with it, or try to ride it like a horse. Err on the side of caution, and always remind your kids to be gentle with the Great Dane. You can never fully predict how your dog will react; a sudden aggressive snap or nip can cause fatal injuries that may require you to rush to the emergency room.

Great Danes can have sudden outbursts of energy known as "zoomies." It may start running around the house at full speed, and can knock your toddler unconscious if he or she stands in the way!

Getting Along with Other Pets – Great Danes and Cats

Some Great Danes may still have retained their prey drive and may see smaller animals as something they can hunt. If you have cats, rabbits or other small animals, Great Danes may chase these around and trap them with its massive paws!

Each dog will respond differently to other pets in the house. You need to socialize them early on to prevent any harm and to avoid your home from becoming a disaster area. It may take a couple of weeks and months for all the animals to settle in and get along with each other.

It may be sensible to provide your cat with spaces where your Great Dane cannot reach it. These can serve as refuges for your cat, and keep it from getting hurt. Installing an appropriately-sized baby gate may also provide a division and space for the animals.

Popular Great Dane Puppy Names

When choosing a name for your Great Dane, it is wiser to stick to shorter ones that the dog can easily remember. You're going to be using it a lot, especially during training, so ensure you pick one that you can easily say and use as a command.

See the table below for popular Great Dane puppy names:

Apollo	Boomer
Attila	Boone
Hulk	Kong
Roman	Shark
Jabba	Lincoln
Rugby	Sammy
Jaws	Bruno
Samson	Mac
Jupiter	Brutus
Saturn	Mack
Bismarck	Magnum
Sergeant	Tank

Burly

Manley

Tex

Thunder

Max

Chunky

Maxi

Titan

Moose

Dragon

Duke

Rosie

CHAPTER 3

Great Dane Supplies – What Do You Need?

Part of your responsibility as a Great Dane owner is to provide it with supplies that will make it happy and comfortable living with you. There are some items you will need to secure, and this chapter will cover those. Some of these things require specific measurements that will make it suitable for a Great Dane, such as dog beds, crates, and kennels. Other things are Great Dane-specific, like elevated feeding bowls to help prevent digestive problems. You should expect to pay more for these items, because of their larger size.

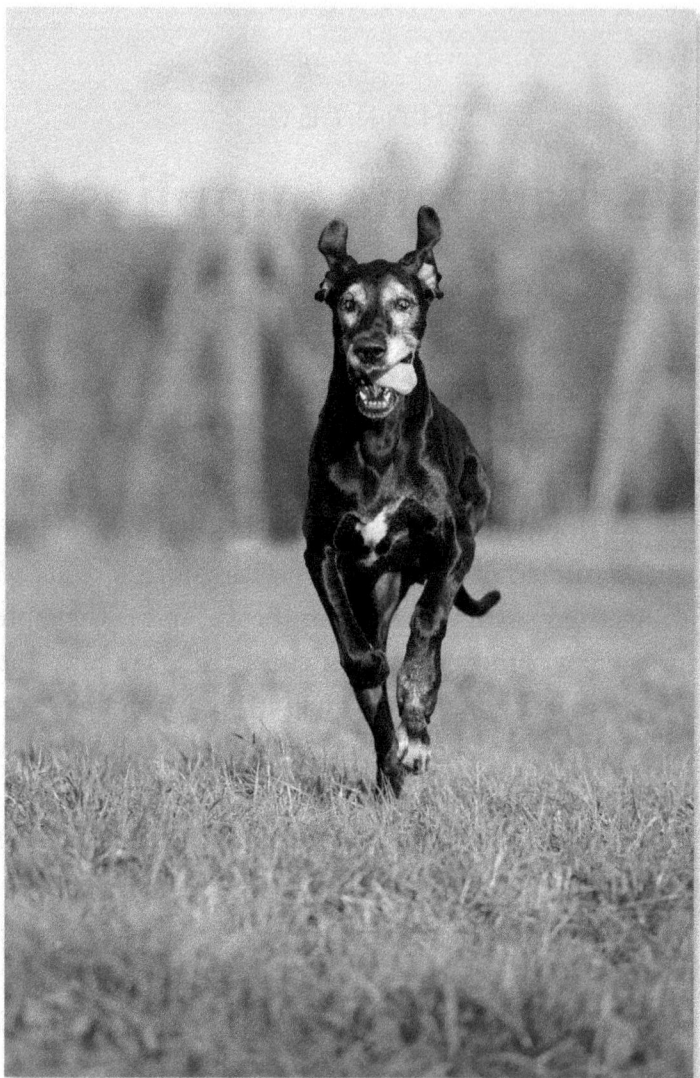

It's your responsibility as a Great Dane owner, to provide your dog with the supplies that will make it happy and comfortable.

Great Dane Dog Food – What Is the Best Food for Great Danes And What Should You Consider When Buying It?

Large breeds like the Great Dane have certain aspects of nutrition that owners need to address. You need to consider in what form the food will come, i.e., kibble, canned, or raw. You should also consider the food quality, protein, and fat levels. It is best to choose high-quality premium dog food.

Go for a light and lean diet for your Great Dane until it is about two years old. Sufficient protein levels in your dog's food can help prevent health problems, such as wobblers syndrome (a disease of the cervical spine that occurs in large breeds such as the Great Dane). The ideal protein level is no higher than 24%, and fat levels range from 12% to 14%.

Provide your Great Dane with an elevated dog feeder to help prevent digestive problems. Allow your dog to rest for at least 45 minutes before exercising it, to avoid bloat.

Great Dane Puppy Food – What Should You Get for This Age?

Be cautious about the food you give to your Great Dane puppy. Large breed formulas often have high levels of protein and fat, that are too much for a growing Great Dane.

Natural premium dog food ensures steady growth and stable levels of energy, which can minimize nutrition-related problems. These kinds of dog food often contain the appropriate blend of minerals, protein, meat, antioxidants, probiotics, and fatty acids.

It also provides protein from meat sources and has higher caloric value, compared to low-quality brands. Most of the ingredients are used by the dog's body and can result in lesser waste and smaller stools. It does not contain by-products, fillers, or artificial flavors. It is available in kibble and canned varieties.

Great Dane Dog Beds – Which Are the Best Ones to Make Your Dog Comfortable?

Letting a Great Dane lie on the floor can cause pain in its hips and elbows, which can potentially cause arthritis issues. That is why a dog bed that is at least 7 in. (18 cm.) thick works best to support its body and bone structure.

Since Great Danes are massive dogs, the ideal measurement for a Great Dane dog bed, it is at least 34 by 54 in. (86 by 137 cm.).

Here are some things you need to consider when buying a dog bed for your Great Dane:

- **Shedding.** Great Danes can shed a lot of fur, which tends to stick and scatter everywhere. To prevent this, cover it with a bedsheet to make it easier to clean.
- **Foam material.** The stuffing inside must be made of an excellent and durable quality that can withstand your dog's weight for a long time. See to it that the foam is not too hard or not too limp. Memory foams can be good options.
- **Outer cover.** These should be resistant to moisture retention to help prevent bacteria build-up.
- **Health issues.** Great Danes are susceptible to hip dysplasia, a condition where the joints do not fit appropriately to its hips.

This can make it difficult for the dog to walk. If your dog has this problem, you may consider getting a custom bed, upon your veterinarian's advice.

Great Dane Dog Collars– How Can You Find One That Fits Perfectly?

To get a collar that correctly fits your Great Dane, use a tape measure to measure the circumference around the dog's neck. You must be able to insert your thumb between the tape measure and the neck and be able to move it around. This will give you an idea of what length of collar to get.

Great Danes are susceptible to hip dysplasia, a condition where the joints do not fit appropriately to its hips.

If you have purchased a collar and see that it is too difficult to slide your thumb in, then the collar is too small. It must not hang too loose either. Otherwise, your dog can easily slide it off. You should be able to buckle a perfectly fitted collar in the middle hole. It is vital to purchase one that is durable and can withstand your dog's weight when it pulls during walks.

If you are buying one for your puppy, remember that its size will change as it grows. Thus, it is essential to be able to buckle it in the inner hole at the same time, to prevent the extended collar strap from disturbing the puppy's movement.

Below are different types of collars that are best for various functions:

- **Soft classic collars.** These are typically made of leather or synthetic collar and have a D-ring, where you can attach the leash. This is generally used for walks.

- **Choke collars.** These can be chain, leather, or synthetic. These are often used for training, or for exhibitions in dog shows. It somehow replicates the sensation when a mother dog slightly squeezes her puppies' neck when she disciplines the litter. Be careful of the choke collar's material as it can cause allergic reactions. Most choke collars are made of alloy, and the safest you can get is copper-based called curogan. Bigger chained-collars about 2 in. (5 cm.) reduce the chance of cutting the dog's fur.

- **Pinch collars.** It is advised to use these only during training sessions. They must accurately fit your dog's neck and be positioned immediately behind the ears. They must not hang out or fall down.

- **Exhibition collars.** These are typically used in dog shows. They appear as a thin cord that showcases the dog's physique.

Great Dane Leashes – What Are the Ideal Types and Lengths?

Ideal leash length depends on the purpose you need. For daily walks, a 6-foot (182 cm.) leash should be sufficient. An 8 to 10 feet (243 to 304 cm.) leash can work well during training. The leash should be long enough to allow your dog to rest, but not too long that it gets tangled in it when it walks.

A wider leash will better suit an adult Great Dane. Also, ensure you get one that is sturdy and can endure your Great Dane's strength when it pulls on it. Nylon is one of the materials that you can count on for durability since it is water-resistant and does not break apart easily. Leather tends to get limp when it absorbs water, and when it has been used for a long time.

Great Dane Harnesses – When Should You Use a Harness?

You may consider using a harness if your dog has respiratory problems, or if it incessantly pulls the leash during walks. Collars can put too much pressure on the dog's neck when it tugs on the leash. It can lead to choking and other lethal health conditions. A harness also gives you better control over your Great Dane since it can discourage pulling.

You will need to start early, if you plan on using a harness on your Great Dane. Most dogs dislike the feeling of having it clad on their bodies, so it can be difficult to ensure acceptance if introduced too late.

To find the right size of harness that fits your Great Dane, measure the girth around your dog's chest just behind the front legs. You know that the harness perfectly fits your dog if you can slide two of your fingers under the harness.

Great Dane Dog Kennels – What Is the Best Size?

Kennels can provide a safe space for your Great Dane to play, stretch its legs, and have its privacy. Outdoor enclosures will prevent your dog from wandering off and getting into accidents.

A kennel that is in the largest size range is the best one you can get for your Great Dane. The best kennel size for a Great Dane is at least 54 in. (137 cm.) long and 32 in. (81 cm.) wide. Metal is a preferable material for large dogs that weigh more than 90 lb. (41 kg.).

Great Dane Crate – What Is the Best Size?

When buying a crate for your Great Dane puppy, measure the dog from its chest to the base of its tail, and again to the top of its shoulders. With that measurement in mind, then add four to six inches (10 to 15 cm.), to arrive at a suitable total measurement.

For adult Great Danes, the best size is at least 46 in. (length) x 30 in. (width) x 33 in. (height) (in centimeters, this measurement is 116 x 76 x 83). You may use one size smaller ... if your Great Dane is not as big.

Great Dane Trailers – What Is the Best Size?

If the need arises where you need to travel with your Great Dane on the road, then a trailer is required. It is a great way to keep it from moving and disturbing you during car travels. The sizing method can be the same as for crates (as above).

Great Dane Dog Shampoo – What Is the Best Type?

Dog shampoos are specially created to condition a dog's skin and fur. Never think you can just grab the one that you use on yourself and lather it on your dog's fur.

See if your dog has sensitive or patchy skin. Hypoallergenic and natural varieties tend to be gentler on your dog. These types lessen the likelihood that your dog will have an allergic reaction.

You may also consider using dry shampoo. Great Danes can be a challenge during bath time, and dry shampoos can keep your dog clean and smelling nice until the time comes to give it a full bath. The powder from the dry shampoo absorbs excess oil and dirt. It is massaged into the dog's coat and brushed out afterward.

Great Dane Brushes – Which Type to Choose?

Choose a brush with soft rubber to comb out loose fur when your Great Dane sheds. This takes out the dead hair while avoiding damage to new, incoming fur. Avoid brushes or combs that have harsher teeth. The Great Dane's coat is relatively short, which makes it easy to brush.

Great Dane Dog Houses – How Big Should They Be, and Which Features Should They Have?

The ideal size for a Great Dane dog house is one where the dog can stand and move around comfortably throughout its life. Its dog bed must also fit within the interior of the house, and must be easy enough to remove when it must be cleaned. It should also have space where you can put its food and water bowl. Be sure to clean the interior of the house regularly to prevent mold and fungus from forming.

If you have bought a kennel or crate, this should give you an idea of how big your Great Dane's dog house should be. Having one that is too big can make the environment cold for your Great Dane, while a smaller one can make it feel cramped.

These are some features that the dog house should have:

- **Proper overhang or space on the front.** This can provide shade, channel rainwater away, and prevent it from entering the dog house.
- **Raised flooring.** This can allow air to flow around the house, keeping it cool and dry. It is also a great way to avoid pests, fleas, and other bacterial infestations forming within the bedding and the structure's interior.
- **Wheels.** These can be handy when you need to move the dog house to another area. You can have the detachable type installed beneath the dog house's floor.
- **Water resistance.** For areas which experience heavy rainfall, the dog house must be treated with a non-toxic water-resistant sealant. This can prevent any water from leaking in.

Great Dane Dog Toys – What Are Fun and Stimulating Items for Your Dog?

When choosing toys for your Great Dane, you need to consider the following qualities:

• Toughness

• Durability

• Safety

• Large Design

• Fun and Stimulating

The toy you provide for your dog must be able to keep its attention and offer it with entertainment for an extended period of time. Great Danes can keep themselves amused by chasing a ball on their own. The size of the ball should be big enough that the dog can maneuver and catch it easily. Toys, where you can play fetch with your Great Dane, are also ideal.

The toys must be able to withstand your Great Dane's handling, and should not easily break into pieces that can become choking hazards. Toys, where you can place treats inside, may not be ideal since you need to keep your Great Dane's weight healthy, and overeating can lead to obesity.

Great Dane Puppy Toys – Which Are Appropriate?

The main issue with a Great Dane puppy is that it is teething at this stage of its life. It will seize and gnaw at anything it can get its mouth on. Chew toys that are oversized and durable work perfectly with Great Dane puppies.

Great Dane Treats – Which Are Safe For Your Dog?

Natural treats are best for your Great Dane. Since you will be giving them in small portions and as rewards during training sessions, you need them to be tasty enough to keep your dog interested. Treats with lower calories are preferable, so they won't be adding to your dog's weight. This will also not disrupt your dog's diet, so it can still consume its appropriate food portion during mealtime. You can opt for vegetables or fruits, such as slices of apples or berries, to introduce antioxidants and minerals into the mix.

You can even make your own homemade dog treats. Some ingredients you can use are:

- Liver
- Oat Flour
- Beef or Chicken Broth

Great Dane Muzzles – How Can You Find One That Fits Your Dog?

To find a muzzle that best fits your Great Dane, follow this measurement procedure:

- **Length:** measure from the tip of the nose to the eye line
- **Circumference:** measure around the snout (which is one inch below that eye line)
- **Neck Circumference:** measure around the neck behind the ears
- **Width:** measure the fullest part of the muzzle

- **Height:** open the dog's mouth a little and measure the height of the snout

Muzzles are essential when you need to take your Great Dane to the veterinarian, transport it to another location, or take it to a place where there is going to be a large crowd which can potentially overwhelm your dog. If you know that your Great Dane can become aggressive, it is best to let it wear a muzzle to avoid any injuries to your dog or to other people. Genuine leather is the best type of material since it has the combination of being both softer and more durable, than many other choices. Keep in mind that your dog should not wear the muzzle for extended periods of time, only in situations where it is needed.

Great Dane Saddles – Should You Let Your Dog Wear One?

If you are letting an animal wear a saddle, the general idea is that you are going to let it carry something. A young healthy dog can supposedly carry one-third of its weight. That is probably how much an average toddler weighs. Great Danes can grow so big that they can be the same size as of a young pony! This gives an impression that Great Danes can be ridden like one. However, it is never a good idea to treat a Great Dane in such a manner. Its spine is not built to perform this type of labor. Letting it wear a saddle and allowing your kids to climb on its back can result in devastating skeletal health concerns, not to mention injuring your children too.

CHAPTER 4

Great Dane Training – How Do You Get Started and Succeed?

You will need to be able to maintain control of your Great Dane as you go about your daily life. Thus, it is essential to train your Great Dane. Your dog is a diamond in the rough, and training it is your solution to refine it to become a well-mannered dog. Great Danes are intelligent dogs and respond well to positive reinforcement.

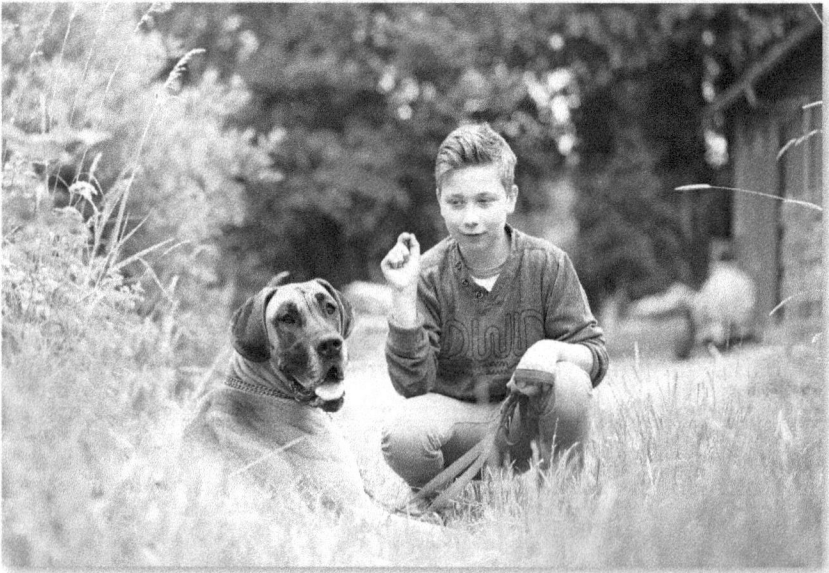

Great Danes are intelligent dogs and respond well to positive reinforcement.

It is important to discover what equipment you need before starting training, and what essential skills and commands you need to master. The Great Dane's puppyhood is the ideal stage to start training. Beginning early will ensure a higher probability of success.

What Are the Things You Need for Great Dane Training?

Before you start training your Great Dane, it's best to have the following items available:

- Leash. To guide and walk your dog; used for obedience training.
- Training collar/harness. It's needed to attach the leash.
- Treats. They are used for positive reinforcement.
- Crate. It is required for crate and potty training.
- Clicker. It is necessary for obedience training.

Great Dane Training Leash

There are two types you can get – 6- feet (182 cm.) and 30-feet (914 cm.) long. The shorter one works for close commands and correction, while a longer leash is used for recall training. You need to ensure that it is sturdy and durable. Nylon is the best type of material for leashes as it can withstand the dog's pulls and exposure to the elements.

Great Dane Training Harness

This is an excellent alternative to collars as it can distribute the pressure all over your dog's body. Harnesses are great training tools for working and guide dogs. These are more efficient when the dog needs to pull something in working environments. Consider skipping the harness if you do not plan to let your Great Dane become a working dog.

Great Dane Dog Treats – Which Are the Best Ones for Positive Reinforcement?

Great Danes are sensitive and respond more to positive reinforcement rather than harsh treatment. Treats are the best way to reward good and obedient behavior, and when your dog has successfully performed a task.

Treats must be tasty to make it enticing for the Great Dane to seek them. You may need to do some trial-and-error to find out what treats excite your dog.

There are two types of treats to remember for their role in your overall training strategy:

- **Low-value.** These are used for average responses.
- **High-value.** If you need a stronger and more interesting lure, or if your dog performed excellently and you feel it deserves a bigger reward.

Training treats must be small so that they can be gobbled quickly, and will not become a distraction during training. You should also be able to carry them around easily in your pocket or in a bait bag. The treats must not also become greasy or crumbly. Remember to choose healthy treats that can maintain your Great Dane's weight.

How to Train a Great Dane – What Skills Must It Learn?

Housebreaking (or potty training): This training is essential if you don't want to clean up after your Great Dane every time and everywhere. Remember, because of the Great Dane's large size, it will excrete bigger stools and larger volumes of urine.

Fix a schedule for feeding times, and remove the dog bowl when meal time is up. This will make your dog excrete all the waste until the next feeding time. After its meals, schedule consistent elimination times and take it out during these periods. When you catch your dog about to defecate … startle it by clapping your hands. And, take it outside immediately. It also helps if you observe signs that may indicate your dog needs to potty, like scratching the floor or door and react accordingly. If your Great Dane has had some accidents inside the house, scrub that particular area thoroughly to get rid of the scent and to prevent the dog from coming back to that spot. Reward your dog with praise and a few treats, if it has successfully relieved itself outside.

Basic dog obedience training: training should begin as early as possible to save it from developing behavior issues.

It should be able to obey commands, such as:

- **Sit.** This command is vital when you need your dog to be calm and still. To do this, grab a treat in your hand and hold it close to the dog's nose. Move your hand upwards and let the dog follow your hand. This will cause its bottom to lower. When it is in a sitting position, say "sit!" so the dog will associate that word with the action. Give it the treat and praise it if it has successfully performed the command.

- **Stay.** This command trains your dog to have self-control. Your Great Dane must have mastered the "sit" command before moving on to this. Order your dog to "sit," and with an open palm, say "sit." Slowly take a few steps back, and give it a reward if it stays in place. You may increase the distance between you and your Great Dane as it masters this command.

- **Come.** In case your dog moves far away from you, or loose grip on the leash, this command will make it come back to you. To do this, put the collar and leash on your dog. Lower yourself to its level, and say "come" while lightly pulling on the leash. When it comes near you, reward it with a treat. Once it has mastered this with the leash, you can take it off and practice it in a safe and enclosed area.

- **Down.** This command makes your dog take on a submissive position, and relaxes it when it is fearful or anxious. Grasping a treat in your hand, make your dog sniff it first, and move your hand slowly to the floor. Make sure your dog is following your movement, and slide your hand along the floor to encourage its body to do the same. Once it is in the "down" position, reward it with the treat, and show praise.

How to Deal with Negative Great Dane Behavior

You will need to assess first what negative behavior your Great Dane is exhibiting. These actions may range from just being a nuisance to being dangerous and harmful. You may need to consult with a certified trainer to see the extent of it, and what are the best training methods that fit your needs. Remember not to overcorrect your Great Dane; start with rewarding positive behavior first.

Great Danes are sensitive and respond more to positive reinforcement rather than harsh treatment.

Starting training early and teaching it proper manners is easier than correcting negative behavior when your Great Dane gets older.

Aggressive Great Danes – Are They a Concern?

Some Great Danes can still display aggression, which is extremely difficult to handle, if you don't know how to respond to them. This can be exhibited through growling and barking. Your Great Dane may lunge at someone or something, and its hundred-pound force can be lethal to whatever its aggression is pointed towards. You will need to address this concern as soon as you can.

Probable causes of aggressive behavior in Great Danes include boredom, separation anxiety, and stress. Removing these factors where possible, may help improve your dog's behavior by removing the root cause.

Great Danes are pack animals, and if they are not socialized correctly, they will see other people and animals as threats. That is why it is absolutely necessary to socialize a Great Dane early on to avoid this problem. See to it that your Great Dane has a consistent socialization schedule, and gradually introduce it to new environments and people. Never force an interaction between your Great Dane and another person or animal if your dog is not yet ready.

Excessive Great Dane Barking

A Great Dane's excessive bark can be a cause for disturbance to your family and neighbors. Its bark is not just a cute squeak that you can ignore until it stops. It is a resounding boom that can echo around your house. It could be that it is demanding your attention and wants something. If you ignore it for a while and give it what it wants, you're only teaching it that it must bark incessantly to acquire what it needs. The only way to remedy this is to let it undergo obedience training and teach it when it is appropriate to bark.

Training for Great Dane Socialization

Socializing your Great Dane is vital for it to become well-mannered. A rowdy and aggressive Great Dane is a dangerous companion to have in your house.

This training is ideal when your Great Dane is still a puppy. Most breeders will keep their pup until after it is seven weeks old. By this time, it has learned how to behave like a dog from its mother and littermates. Ideally, your breeder has slowly introduced the puppy to different people – children, adults, males, and females.

Seek an experienced Great Dane trainer to review your plan for socializing your dog. With your trainer's advice, you can help avoid behavior problems that could be difficult to correct in the future.

You will also need to go to your veterinarian to have the vaccinations your Great Dane requires. Immunizations can protect it from contagious viruses and diseases, such as Canine Parvo Virus.

Below are some things you can do to start socializing your Great Dane:

- **Daily touch.** This will make your dog accustomed to the sensation of a person's contact. Gently stroke your dog on its head. If you see that your dog seems to enjoy your pat, you can then allow your other family members and friends to do the same. Always monitor these interactions between your dog and other people, especially children.
- **Car rides.** It is crucial that your dog will become comfortable in car rides, especially during trips to the veterinarian or to the dog park. Start with short car rides around the neighborhood. Once you see your dog feel at ease, you can gradually increase the length of the trip.

- **Noise.** It is essential that your dog can endure environments with loud noises. If you miss exposing your dog to loud sounds, it may be too difficult to handle your dog when situations arise where loud noises are present. It may get anxious, overwhelmed, or frightened, causing it to exhibit signs of stress. You can start by letting your dog stay in its crate while watching television or playing music.

- **Walks.** Start by walking your dog around your neighborhood. This will help it get used to cars, people, and other animals in the area. Begin with a short ten-minute walk, and gradually increase the length of time when you see your dog grow more comfortable going outside.

- **Crowds.** You may be living in an area densely populated with people, and you will not be able to escape crowds. Your dog must be able to master obedience commands, so you can control it in these situations. It is also best to teach your dog a command where it will bring its focus on you. Find out what makes your dog uncomfortable, and things that can make it overstimulated. Keep your dog close to you when you are in a crowded place.

- **People.** When you are out with your Great Dane, chances are high it will attract other people's attention. Start by allowing one or two interested people to approach your dog and ensure you supervise the interaction.

- **Other animals.** Parks and farms are great places to start acquainting your dog to other animals. Be on guard as it approaches other animals, and use your commands when you see your Great Dane become aggressive or rough.

Can Great Danes Swim? How Can You Train Your Dog to Do So?

There are dog breeds that are natural swimmers, like the Water Spaniel, Golden Retriever, and Newfoundland. These dogs have webbed feet, which make it easy for them to paddle through the water.

Great Danes do not belong to this category. They don't have webbed paws. Instead, they have round, compact feet and strong, well arched-toes.

However, this does not mean to say that you should not allow your Great Dane to swim, or this breed cannot swim at all. Each dog is different, and you will need to find out how it responds when it gets submerged in water.

If you are intent on training your Great Dane to swim, it's always best to start early. You may consider buying safety equipment, like floatation devices that fit your Great Dane. Begin by allowing it to come to a shallow area and see how it reacts to getting wet. Always stay beside your dog at this stage. Support its body, and praise it when you see it does a great job. When your session is over, teach it how to safely exit the area so it can do so on its own the next time.

Great Dane Shock Collar – Does Your Dog Need It for Training?

Shock collars give an electric current of varying intensity. It is used in training as a negative reinforcement. This has become a controversial method in dog training as it can harm the dog's physical and mental well-being. Shock collars have been reported to cause burns on the dog's neck, and induce psychological stress.

Great Danes are sensitive dogs. Using a shock collar is too harsh for them, and can make the dog distrustful and anxious. Shock collars must only be handled by expert trainers. Insisting on using one for your Great Dane without the right knowledge and using it in the wrong circumstances can make your training ineffective. This breed is intelligent and responds more to positive reinforcement.

CHAPTER 5

Great Dane Puppies and Great Dane Adults for Sale

H ow much does a Great Dane cost? One thing is for sure – a massive dog demands a hefty price tag. The price will include the breeder's efforts from the time of copulation, pregnancy, and the birth of the puppies. With the knowledge you have of Great Danes so far, you know that its needs are supersized and require larger amounts of supplies.

You need to be careful where you buy your Great Dane. This will ensure that the dog you get is healthy, and you have all the support you need to raise it.

You need to be careful where you buy your Great Dane. This will ensure that the dog you get is healthy, and you have all the support you need to raise it.

Adult Great Dane Price – How Much Is?

Most breeders start their prices at USD $1000. Great Danes with pedigrees and papers will cost more.

Great Dane Price Ranges – What Should You Expect?

Price ranges for Great Danes do vary. The overall range is usually between USD $600 to $3,000. This breed is considered a luxury, so you will need to prepare to pay approximately this amount. The average cost you will spend on care for the dog's first year, is around USD $3,500.

Buying a Great Dane – What Are the Things You Should Avoid?

Avoid breeders who have puppies available for sale throughout the year. Responsible breeders do not allow their dams to produce more than two to three litters in a year. Don't buy from a breeder who is willing to ship their puppies to a given address. Responsible breeders need to meet aspiring Great Dane owners to assess how qualified a person is to take care of the dog. Stay away from breeders who sell oversized or undersized dogs, or people who market their dogs as "rare." These dogs may already have pre-existing health conditions.

Great Dane Puppies – Where Should You Look for One?

You should only buy Great Dane puppies from reputable and responsible breeders. Buying from a breeder who is knowledgeable and is genuinely concerned about the puppies' health contributes to the overall longevity of the dogs. Avoid buying puppies from puppy mills, pet stores, and backyard breeders who do not know of any ethical standards.

Buying A Great Dane Puppy – What Are the Questions to Ask?

Before visiting your chosen kennel and discussing with the breeder, you need to have the following questions ready:

1. **"How many years have you been taking care and breeding Great Danes?"** Ideally, the breeder must have at least three to four years of experience handling and breeding Great Danes.

2. **"What Great Dane clubs are you part of?"** A reputable breeder must be a member of an AKC (American Kennel Club) or CKC (Canadian Kennel Club) - an affiliated organization for at least three to four years and have regularly participated in dog shows. Another club the person can join is the Great Dane Club of America. Membership in these organizations supports the breeder's claim that he or she has extensive knowledge and experience with Great Danes.

3. **"Do you have any dog show experience?"** Inquire what types of dog shows the breeder has participated in. Ask for any certificate of participation, and any other awards the dogs have received.

4. **"What training have you done with the dog? Are there any skills you are working on with it?"** Socialization must be on top of the breeder's list on the training he or she has done with the dog. He or she should also have started with housebreaking. The breeder must give you sound advice on how you can continue the training he or she started.

5. **"Are there any health concerns in the puppies' lineage?"** The breeder must be honest in discussing any health issues that may potentially arise. He or she must also be aware of any congenital and contracted diseases a Great Dane can have. Ask about the best time to give the dog vaccinations.

6. **"How is the health of the parents?"** Find out if the parents have regular check-ups for health conditions. Ask who dogs' veterinarians are.

7. **"Can you show me the puppies' registration papers and health certificates?"** He or she must be ready to present these to you. It is mandatory for a reputable breeder to turn over a four-generation AKC pedigree certificate when you are purchasing a Great Dane puppy.

8. **"Do you have a warranty for the dog?"** Is the breeder willing to take the dog back in case you are unable to care for it? Will he or she also give any guarantee should any health issues arise, and willing to sign an agreement? These terms can vary for different breeders.

9. **"Do you have any references from past clients?"** The person must be ready to give you a list of references of owners who bought their Great Danes from them. Contact them as soon as possible and ask how their puppies are doing, if they

have observed any health concerns, and how the transaction process with the breeder went.

10. **Lastly, "what is the price for your Great Dane puppy?"** Now, this is for you as an aspiring Great Dane owner. Does the price that the breeder specified fit your budget? You will also need to ask him or her other estimated expenses you may incur, for the care and maintenance of the puppy. In this way, you will have a good idea of the total cost on a yearly basis.

You will also need to see the puppies' living environment. Is it clean and safe? Dogs who grow in filthy surroundings are often difficult to housebreak. Responsible breeders also never sell their puppies under seven weeks of age. They also ensure the puppies have had their vaccines and deworming before their new families welcome them home. It is also best to go to a veterinarian and have the puppy checked before finalizing the sale. To officially seal the deal, make sure all agreements are in writing and in a signed contract.

CHAPTER 6

Great Dane Breeding – What Are the Important Things to Keep in Mind?

A breeder's main goal is to help improve the breed. This means the breeder takes due diligence in his or her research and efforts to make sure the puppies produced by their dogs are top quality and have excellent temperaments. They should do everything they can to minimize, if not eliminate, health conditions that can be passed on to the puppies.

Becoming a Great Dane breeder is a big responsibility. It is important to be informed so that you can make good decisions to ensure your dog will have a healthy and happy life.

Breeding Great Danes is a serious responsibility. If you plan on becoming a Great Dane breeder, you must be prepared to provide and perform all the necessary requirements to ensure your dog produces a healthy litter.

Great Dane Breeders – What Are the Signs You Should Know of a Responsible One?

A "breeder" is any person who conducts the breeding of two dogs to produce a litter and owns the female dog. You will need to be diligent in researching breeders who sell Great Danes. It is vital to discern if the breeder is reputable and responsible. Some of them are backyard breeders, others operate in puppy mills, while others recklessly allow their dogs to breed without considering health issues. The breeder must comply with the Great Dane

Club of America's "Breeder's Code of Ethics." This serves as a guideline for them to ensure the puppies produced from their breeding pair are healthy.

Reputable breeders often participate in dog shows and are members of at least one Great Dane club. Be careful of breeders who claim to sell show-quality dogs, but have not even participated in one!

Here are more qualities you need to look out for when choosing a breeder to buy your Great Dane from:

- They need to be knowledgeable about the breed. You can find this out by asking the right questions.
- They openly discuss the pros and cons of Great Dane ownership. They don't only tell you the good things about the breed to convince you to shell out your cash.

When visiting the breeder's kennel, keep in mind these criteria so that you can make an informed decision on the selection of the breeder to work with:

- Are the surroundings clean?
- Is the kennel clean, odor-free, and well structured?
- Are the adult dogs groomed, well-fed, and taken care of?
- How do the dogs interact with another? Do they seem healthy, friendly, and active?
- You should be able to see the breeding pair, or at least the dam. Check its temperament. If it is too aggressive, anxious or

frightful, there is a good chance the puppies will also turn out like their mom.

Below are some qualities the breeding Great Dane pair must have:

- The parents must be AKC (American Kennel Club) registered. This will assure you that the dog is purebred. The breeder must have these certifications before they are allowed their dogs to breed, or else their puppies will be ineligible for registration.
- The adult dogs and puppies must look like the breed they represent! Show-quality dogs will have better conformation, and you must be able to recognize that it is a Great Dane immediately. Some breeders may be dishonest, and won't disclose if the puppies are from a mixed-breed pair. Other litters are produced from a lineage of poor quality breeding that they hardly look like Great Danes at all! Buyer beware, so the information presented in this book should help you discern the correct look for a Great Dane, as mentioned earlier in this book.
- They should at least have the coat colors that adhere to the AKC standard.
- They should have excellent, stable temperaments, and are in optimal physical condition.

Responsible breeders also do many pre-breeding health exams to ensure their dogs will not pass any hereditary diseases to their litters. They should even have their breeding stock undergo routine health check-ups. Always require papers and health certificates from the breeder.

Here are some necessary health exams the breeder must have allowed their Great Dane to undergo:

- X-ray and have the dogs receive a certification from the Orthopedic Foundation for Animals (OFA) or Penn HIP against hip dysplasia and other joint and bone disorders. OFA is comprised of a panel of veterinarians who screen x-ray results.
- Eye exams and have a Canine Eye Registration Foundation certificate declaring healthy eyes or free from any heritable diseases.
- Thyroid tests and have normal results.
- The pair should be parasite free.
- Tested negative against brucellosis, a contagious disease that can lead to infertility in breeding stocks.

Female Great Dane - How Can You Prepare Her for Breeding?

If you are planning to become a Great Dane breeder, you must be the owner of the female (called the "bitch"). Kennel clubs recognize the owner of the female dog as the breeder. It is ideal that she is mated to another Great Dane that is registered in the American Kennel Club or Canadian Kennel Club. It is always the breeder's goal to produce excellent, healthy, good-tempered, and long-lived Great Danes.

Becoming a Great Dane breeder is a big responsibility. You will need to make informed decisions to ensure your dog, and its litters, will have a healthy and happy life. The first choice you need to make is if you are getting a Great Dane for the purpose of breeding. It takes years of experience to know which combinations of breeding pairs produce the best litter and the specific coat you desire.

You will need to assess your bitch's health and think carefully about her robustness. Even if your dog has a champion title, this does not guarantee that she should be bred. Be open to consulting other breeders if you are not sure about your evaluation. Your female Great Dane requires long-term care, which breeders refer to as conditioning. This involves regular visits to the veterinarian for check-ups, screening for any inheritable genetic issues, regular exercise, and proper nutrition. Working with your veterinarian and another breeder, you will be able to search for a mate that can help eliminate or balance out identified health concerns. Your female Great Dane should not be overweight and have good muscle tone before breeding.

Female Great Danes grow to sexual maturity when she reaches six to nine months of age. You need to know the different stages of this period:

- **Proestrus.** She will have a bloody vaginal discharge, and her vulva will become swollen. This period will typically last for nine days, and she will not be receptive to mating.
- **Estrus.** She will become fertile and will be open to a male for mating. This will also have a duration of nine days. Ovulation happens in the first 48 hours.

- **Diestrus.** This stage ends the mating period when your dog will no longer be receptive to a male. This will often last for 60 to 90 days. Vaginal discharges turn back to bright red, and the swelling of the vulva will reduce.
- **Anestrus.** Sexual hormones are at low levels during this time that lasts for four to five months.

You must also be knowledgeable about the Great Dane Club of America Breeder's Code of Ethics. It specifies that the breeder must maintain the best possible standards of health, cleanliness, safety, and care for their dogs. Breeders must not alter their Great Dane's appearance, physique, condition, or natural temperament of the dog by any means other than what is allowed in the Official Breed Standard.

Male Great Dane – How Can You Prepare Him for Breeding?

If you own a male Great Dane, you should also decide if you will allow him to mate. Do not make a reckless mistake of letting it breed with a female Great Dane without doing the necessary steps to ensure it can sire healthy puppies.

Male Great Danes will also reach sexual maturity around six to nine months of age. They should also be subject to the same rigorous health exams as females. One health condition he should be regularly tested for is a brucellosis test. Brucellosis is a bacterial infection, usually from dairy-related products. If you fail to do this, and the disease is introduced to a kennel, it can be easily contracted by the other dogs and can cause widespread sterility and abortion, which causes the damage of an excellent breeding kennel.

Female Great Danes grow to sexual maturity when they reaches six to nine months of age.

The veterinarian should also evaluate his scrotum, testicles, penis, and prepuce. A semen analysis should also be conducted to assess your dog's fertility. Also, work with them to find out the best diet and exercise to keep your male Great Dane healthy and fit for breeding.

Great Dane Stud – How Can You Take Care, And Look for One?

A Great Dane stud is a registered dog retained for breeding. This implies that the dog is not neutered and is capable of siring litters.

See the section above on how you can take care of a male Great Dane and prepare him for breeding.

If you want to establish yourself as an owner of a quality Great Dane stud, you must have him registered in the American Kennel Club or Canadian Kennel Club. Participating in dog shows is a way to showcase your Great Dane, have him earn championship titles to certify he has great conformation and excellent qualities, and to connect with other breeders.

Another concern you need to put your attention to is the temperature of the environment your stud dog is living in. When the surroundings exceed the body's normal temperature, his fertility can be compromised. If the dog suffers from overheating, the stored sperm in his testicles can die. It can take 60 days for the sperm to be replaced. You will need to manage the temperature to keep the dog's sperm alive and healthy.

Do not reprimand your male Great Dane when you see him exhibiting mounting behavior. You may feel embarrassed seeing him doing this, especially if you have guests around. Giving him this response will make him hesitant to mount a bitch, or dismounts when he sees you near him. Keeping his dewclaws may also be a good idea. This will help him have a better grip on the female, which increases the chances of a successful tie.

Check any puppies that he has sired, along with their dams. See their characteristics and temperament. Discuss with the breeder how their stud was able to complement any faults with the bitches he has bred with.

Once you have chosen a Great Dane stud for your female, arrange to meet him in person. Great Dane stud listings can sometimes involve pictures that have been enhanced, and may not accurately reflect the dog's actual condition. Ask the breeder for the dog's genetic results.

After you have done all the necessary health exams, genetic screenings, and selected a suitable mate for your bitch, the next thing you need to do is to create a contract with the stud's owner. This should be done before the copulation takes place. All obligations and circumstances of both parties must be clearly stated in writing. This must be signed by all parties involved in the transaction.

The stud's owner arranges the fee. He or she may ask for a cash fee, "pick of the litter," or one or more puppies from the resulting litter.

New Born Pups – What to Feed a Great Dane Puppy?

The mother's milk is still the best food new-born puppies can have. Her milk can keep the puppies nourished, even if her health fails. The challenge is how you can provide proper nutrition for the mother dog that will allow her to supply milk to her litter, and at the same time, keep her healthy.

A large breed like the Great Dane requires producing more milk daily. Because milk production is such a high energy-consuming process, it is recommended that the level of metabolized energy (ME) she gets be increased to 200%. This translates to doubling her food intake before she was bred and must be done soon after whelping. The ME should be increased to 300% during lactating peaks, usually three to four weeks post-whelping. The easiest way to provide this large number of calories is to feed her with "performance" type dog food. This is designed for working dogs and has a very high energy level in a highly dense digestible formula. Consult with your veterinarian to know the appropriate diet to give to your Great Dane to meet these requirements.

CHAPTER 7

Great Dane Adoption – What Are the Crucial Things to Consider?

The reasons why a Great Dane ends up in rescue shelters are always unfortunate. However, as an aspiring Great Dane owner, one of the greatest and most soul-satisfying things you can do is to adopt one. Not only have you saved it from a grim fate of being in line for euthanasia, but you have also provided it with a loving home and a second chance at life. Great Danes from shelters often have traumatic experiences that they carry as a burden. This can impact their behavior and responses to you, over time. You will need to know how to care for individuals like these, in order to help them heal from their traumatic pasts. You can also contribute to helping save Great Danes, by becoming a foster parent.

A large breed like the Great Dane produces more milk (lactates) than a smaller breed.

Great Dane Rescue – What Happened to These Dogs?

There are some reasons why Great Danes end up in rescue shelters. People often make the hasty decision to get a Great Dane without fully understanding what the dog's needs are. They did not do their research, thus making them unprepared when the dog reaches its full size. Others find out they cannot afford to provide for the dog's needs. Sometimes, circumstances happen in the family, such as divorce, a new baby, or having to move to another home, make it difficult for the owners to continue caring for their Great Dane.

These Great Danes end up as strays who were left to fend for themselves after their owners abandoned them. Other dogs were surrendered to rescue shelters after realizing they can no longer care for their pet. Whatever the reason is behind their presence in the rescue shelter, they all share the same fate: they will likely be euthanized if no one will claim or adopt them. Rescue shelters have only limited space and resources to care for all the dogs that come to them. As much as they want to care for all the dogs that they rescue, it is impossible to care for every dog when they have reached their maximum capacity. As a way to manage the population, they oftentimes must resort to this method.

Great Dane Puppy Rescue – How to Take Care of a Rescued Dog?

Caring for a rescue dog will not be easy. Your decision to adopt it has saved its life, but you will need to deal with any emotional trauma your puppy may have.

Below are ways you can take care of your rescued Great Dane puppy:

- **Be patient.** Your Great Dane puppy may have been trapped living in undesirable conditions for a long time. This probably affected the dog negatively, and so it may show signs of aggression or fear. Don't push any interactions with other people if you see that your dog is not ready. You will need to spend time with it and be gentle with your verbal and non-verbal language.

- **Make your dog feel safe.** Providing your dog with a crate may help it feel safe, as it considers this space a place to retreat to. You can make it comfortable for the dog by providing bedding and leaving the door of the crate open. Be careful not to make sudden, loud noises that can frighten it, especially yelling. Speak in soft, soothing tones.

- **Prepare for any health problems.** Dogs from rescue shelters may suffer from health conditions including heart disease, kidney problems, hyperthyroidism, deafness, and eye problems. Shelters usually treat medical conditions, along with spaying or neutering them. However, there may be health issues that the shelter was not able to discover, and you will need to prepare for the cost of having it treated.

Great Dane Rescue Locations

There are many Great Dane rescue shelters that can be found in the United States, Canada, and the United Kingdom. Some rescue shelters focus on the geographical location, while others concentrate on rescuing a specific breed. The resource list that is included in this book will give you some locations where you can find rescued Great Danes.

Great Danes For Adoption Near Me – Where Can I Find Them?

Doing a search online will be the easiest way to narrow your choices of finding an adoption shelter near you. One website that can help you do this is Petfinder http://www.petfinder.com.

However, keep in mind that you will need to visit these shelters and check out the dogs personally. You need to see the environment where the dog is living and how it interacts with the others. You will also need to assess if the shelter is a reputable one that has procedures in place in taking care of their rescued dogs.

When visiting rescue shelters, it is best to avoid the afternoons or weekends. These are times when shelters get crowded, and this can overwhelm the animals. If you need to spend more time evaluating the perfect Great Dane from the rescue shelter, it is best to come during the middle of the week.

Great Dane Rescue – How Can You Help?

Great Dane Rescue Inc., whose website is: http://www.greatdane rescueinc.com welcomes persons who love the breed and are willing to care for them to join their foster team. Great Danes typically do not behave well in kennels, and their foster system lets volunteers provide home environments for their rescued Great Dane. Volunteers also help evaluate the dog's behavior and habit. They will be able to know the dog better, thus provide more information on how to match it with potential families who plan to adopt them.

You will also need to say goodbye to them when their adoptive family comes to take them. The organization has created counter-measure procedures for anyone becoming a foster parent as a way of by-passing the organization's adoption process.

It takes a great sense of responsibility and commitment to be a Great Dane "foster parent." Below are some things you need to know if you plan on becoming one:

- **Commitment and responsibility.** You will need to provide the Great Dane with all the care and attention it requires, and for however long it needs to stay with you. You will need to exercise, feed, groom, socialize and train it with necessary skills and commands.

- **Time fostering the Great Dane may vary.** It may be as short as one day, or as long as several months. It will all depend on the dog, its personality, age, health, and other factors. Dogs that are younger than two years old typically do not stay with a foster family for a long time.

- **Space.** A fenced yard is preferable, but not necessary. Fenced yards give the rescued Great Dane the safest possible environment when it needs to exercise and relieve itself.

- **Time.** You must be able to spend at least two hours with the dog every day. Dogs who have spent more time with their foster parents have been seen to become more prepared for placement quickly. There may be some dogs who need more than two hours of your time every day, especially if they have had traumatic experiences and need more care. Any time you will not be available to look after the dog during the day, the organization requires that it must be leashed or confined in a secure area, preferably in a crate. Should you need to go on a vacation or travel for your job, you need to be prepared to create a support system in your absence. Other foster parents have arranged for a pet sitter, or have asked their family members to help take care of the dog while they were out of town.

- **Expenses.** You will have to buy the rescued Great Dane quality dog food to keep it nourished, and toys to keep it entertained. The GDRI will pay for the treatment of some medical concerns, including heartworm preventative treatment.

If you are ready to become a foster parent, visit the Great Dane Rescue Inc. website and fill out their volunteer application form. They will contact you for a phone screening, and if you meet their preliminary requirements, along with the completed volunteer application, their staff will get in touch with you and schedule a home visit. They will also provide more detailed information regarding your responsibilities as a foster parent, and answer any queries you may have.

CHAPTER 8

Living with Your Great Dane

What can you do to make living conditions for your Great Dane healthy and safe? This section will give you tips on practical measures you can do to make living with your Great Dane more harmonious and efficient. Discover how you can determine the best spot to place your Great Dane dog house and bed, and other considerations you may need to take into account. There are some items that you need to install in your house to make your Great Dane safe, such as dog gates and childproof latches. Part of being a responsible Great Dane owner is ensuring you have done all that you can to make living conditions with your dog and other family members healthy and safe.

Part of being a responsible Great Dane owner is ensuring you have done all that you can to make living conditions suitable for the dog, and yourself.

Great Dane Savvy Owner – How Can You Become One?

Becoming a Great Dane-savvy owner will enable you to have the knowledge and experience to handle your dog better.

Below are some tips on how you can become one:

- **Be prepared for emergencies.** It is essential that you know how to perform first aid for your Great Dane in case it gets into an accident or sudden illness. Should your dog need to be taken to the veterinarian, have a protocol in place on how you can make it there, especially if you will not be around when emergency situations occur.

- **Stay active together.** Your Great Dane will need its daily exercise to keep it healthy and to maintain its weight. Another reason why this is important is that it strengthens your bond with the dog. Find exciting ways to keep you and yourself moving. Remember that allowing your Great Dane to become overweight will be severely detrimental to its health.

Great Dane Puppies – How Can You Prepare Your Home for Them?

Before you welcome your new Great Dane puppy into your home, you will need to prepare your family, and the physical requirements in your home to allow the dog to live with you safely.

It can be overwhelming for your new Great Dane puppy to be introduced to a new environment. Let it wear its collar and leash, and give it a tour around your home, one room at a time when it first arrives. This is also a great time to establish your dominance, as the dog will begin to see you as the leader. Slowly introduce other members of your family to the dog, and give them a heads up to not become rough or overly excited. It may be tempting for your family to rush in and shower the new pup with hugs and kisses.

If you have already done shopping for Great Dane supplies, strategically position them in the areas of your house. This includes its feeding and water bowl and the dog bed. It should be placed where your dog can easily access it. The dog bed and feeding bowls should not be placed near each other. The bed must not be positioned near items that can potentially harbor bacteria and mold.

It can be helpful if you puppy-proof your home before you welcome your Great Dane. As it grows, your Great Dane will be able to reach kitchen counters and will be able to grab the food you place on it. Train it early on, that this is not acceptable behavior. Install childproof latches on drawers and cabinets to prevent your dog from opening and tampering with cleaning supplies and other potentially dangerous chemicals. Your Great Dane will gravitate to any object that resembles your scent, and any of your expensive items could potentially be perceived as a personal chew toy as a result! Store any expensive belongings securely, when your dog is unsupervised for long periods.

Great Dane Dog Cages– Are They a Good Idea?

Humans and dogs have different perspectives when it comes to cages and crates. We may see it as a prison, but for dogs who were positively introduced to it, they see the cage as a safe place. Their natural denning instinct makes them feel protected when they are in enclosed spaces. Dogs in the wild spend up to 16 hours resting to save their energy for essential activities, such as hunting. Puppies need a place to escape when the house gets too rowdy and noisy.

You must also balance the time the puppy spends inside the cage. Do not leave it alone and isolated for a long time. It will need time to interact and socialize with other family members and animals in your house.

The cage must be large enough that your Great Dane can fit inside without having to crumple itself like a pretzel. It should allow the dog to stand naturally, lie on its side and stretch its legs, and quickly turn around. A properly-sized crate can also help you in housebreaking it. Dogs typically do not relieve themselves in places where they sleep.

The crate can also facilitate the puppy when it is teething and needs to chew to relieve the pain. It will find a place where it can chew without being disturbed. Chewing in a "den" allows it to exercise its natural instinct of eating in its den after a hunt. This also protects your furniture and other things in your house from being destroyed by a teething Great Dane.

You can also use the cage as a "time-out" space if your Great Dane is behaving beyond your control. Allow it to enter the crate without scolding it. Be careful not to create any negative associations between the dog and the crate. If you do, it will become difficult to coax the dog in, should another situation arise where you need contain it. The duration of these time-outs does not need to be long; they can be as short as ten minutes. Doing this allows the dog to bring his behavior under control, in a non-threatening environment.

The crate can also be used as a management tool. Dog trainers typically divide management into two aspects: training and management. Training is the process of correcting the dog's behavior while managing your dog involves avoiding negative behavior altogether. You can train your dog to enter the crate and start chewing when you have guests in your house. Crate management can be used to anticipate behavioral problems, such as destructive chewing, nipping at children, and house soiling.

As long as your Great Dane has met its social and physical requirements, a good rule of thumb is that it can stay inside the crate overnight, and up to half the day. Keep in mind that it is vital for your puppy to be socialized during this stage in its life, so make sure that its time outside the crate involves positive interaction with other people.

Great Dane Kennels – Do You Need One for Your Dog?

If you have a yard big enough to let your Great Dane run around, a kennel is a good idea to place in that space. This will prevent the dog from escaping, thus keeping it safe from any road accidents. This should be strong enough not to break when your Great Dane attempts to break it or leans on it.

Great Dane Dog House – Where to Place It If You Get One?

There are many things to consider when you are planning to provide a dog house for your Great Dane. The most important factor is it must be the right size for your dog and made of quality materials. It must also be able to withstand the climate you live in.

It is essential to plan where to place the dog house. Its position can affect your dog's comfort and health. It all boils down to being observant and paying attention to how your home responds to the elements.

Never put the dog house in a spot where it will be directly exposed to sunlight for more than a couple of hours during the day. This is important especially if you plan to let the dog stay inside for an extended period. To find out where a shady spot is, spend a day in your yard and observe a couple of places that are shaded throughout most of the day.

Considering wind exposure is essential especially during the fall and winter months. The dog house may be ravaged by cold winds. You need to pay attention to where the doghouse is facing. Its orientation must not face the direction where the strongest winds are blowing from. You need to observe again where the wind is coming from. If your climate is typically chilly or windy, you may even consider insulating the dog house.

Soil drainage is a vital factor to deal with. When heavy rainfall comes, your yard must not become full of standing water. Observe where water tends to gather, and avoid positioning the doghouse there. If you see that your whole yard has a drainage problem, the elevating of the dog house can be a possible solution. This can be done by placing wheels on it or positioning it on a taller platform. Another solution to improve soil drainage is laying down sand or gravel before you construct the dog house.

After you have handled all the fundamental components of the dog house, you can move on to dealing with the practical and aesthetic concerns. What would be the easiest method of letting your dog go inside and outside the doghouse? How can it easily access the yard? Can the dog go to the house on its own, or is it part of a kennel? Aesthetically, you should consider how the dog house will blend with your own home environment.

Great Dane Dog Beds – Where Are the Best Places to Put Them?

Your Great Dane will demand a lot of space especially when they have reached full size. You will need to position its dog bed in an area where it can still have a lot of surrounding open space. Keep their sleeping area free from any fragile items and furniture. This will keep them safe from smacking on to these things and protect them from injury and damage to your belongings.

You may also consider placing it in a corner or below an open staircase. It gives the dog the feeling of being protected and enclosed. Also, it's important to position the dog bed in an area that is not too busy but will still be able to be within earshot of family members. Keep the temperature of its sleeping space comfortable; not too hot nor too cold. You may consider providing a heating pad if it gets too chilly but of course, carefully supervise this. Do not place the dog bed in the same area of its dog bowl; its sleeping area must always be kept clean.

Great Dane Dog Door – What Is the Ideal Size?

*Your Great Dane will demand a lot of space, especially
when it has reached full-size adulthood.*

Dog doors make it convenient for your Great Dane to come in and out of your house whenever it pleases. This is especially important when your dog must relieve itself outside. An ideal size for a dog door that fits a Great Dane is at least 16 x 23 3/4 in. (41 x 60 cm.). You can choose to have a flap dog door, a hard-plastic dog door which you can lock, or a magnetic door which can be unlocked when the dog wearing a unique collar comes near it.

Great Dane Dog Gates – Does Your House Need One?

Having a dog gate for your Great Dane is an efficient way to set boundaries in your house. There may be specific areas in your home that you want to keep off-limits to your dog in certain situations. This is essential since Great Danes have the tendency to lean on people, and unconsciously knock down small children. One thing you need to remember when getting a dog gate for your Great Dane is that it must be sturdy and well-constructed, so that it will not easily break when your dog applies its substantial weight, during opening.

Should You Allow Your Dog to Lay on the Couch?

Letting your Great Dane sit on the sofa or bed gives them the idea that it is equal or above its owner, in the pack hierarchy. It will also think that it is acceptable behavior. This may also lead to your Great Dane becoming territorial over the sofa. This means it may show signs of aggression when you attempt to sit on the couch that it has come to see as its territory. This can be dangerous when you have guests, and they are not aware of your dog's behavior. It may also exhibit the same attitude when you bring your Great Dane to your friend or relative's house.

Another reason not to let your Great Dane sit on the sofa is to keep its mess, dirt, and loose hair off it, especially if your dog has been outside. This can prevent the spread of bacteria and prevent parasitic infections, for everyone living in your house.

If your dog is already used to sitting on the couch, it is not too late to rectify this. Begin by training it with obedience commands, such as sit, stay, and down. Redirect your dog elsewhere, every time it attempts to sit on the sofa. Consistency and repetition are essential to imprint positive behavior in this area.

CHAPTER 9

Great Dane Health – What Should You Know?

Great Danes are susceptible to many health problems, and these can be fatal if not immediately attended to. These range from orthopedic problems, eye issues, and skin complications. Great Danes already have a short lifespan compared to other dogs, and these medical conditions further endanger their lives. You will also need to guard your Great Dane against contagious diseases, such as Canine Parvo Virus and distemper, by giving it necessary vaccinations. Following this advice will help you prevent these conditions, save your dog a lot of pain, and you will find prevention is much less expensive than finding cures!

Great Danes are susceptible to many health problems that can be fatal, if not immediately attended to.

Great Dane Health Concerns – What Are the Common Problems for This Breed?

There are a number of health concerns that your Great Dane may suffer from that you need to prepare for. This breed is the most likely of all dogs to have an emergency gastrointestinal syndrome called bloat. This serious health condition can kill your Great Dane within hours. Great Danes are also susceptible to cardiomyopathy and cancer, especially bone cancer. Orthopedic problems are also common, such as hip dysplasia, osteochondritis (inflammation within a joint of the bone or cartilage), hypertrophic osteodystrophy (improper growth of a bone), luxating patella (kneecaps that have moved out of the proper location), panosteitis (bone inflammation), and wobbler syndrome (cervical spine condition causing abnormal walking).

Common eye diseases that Great Danes can have are cataracts (clouding of the cornea), eyelid abnormalities, cherry eye, glaucoma, and Progressive Retinal Atrophy (PRA). Some of the hormonal disorders your Great Dane can develop are hypothyroidism and Addison's disease. Your Great Dane may also be vulnerable to skin diseases which include: allergies, folliculitis (inflammation of the hair follicles), furunculosis (infection of the hair follicles causing abscesses), demodectic mange (caused by mites), calcinosis (depositing of calcium in the skin), and in blue Danes, color dilution alopecia (genetic hair loss).

Other medical concerns in Great Danes include epilepsy, blood-clotting disease (von Willebrand's), and Megaesophagus (enlargement of the esophagus). Harlequin Danes are especially susceptible to inherited deafness.

Wobblers Great Dane – What Are the Symptoms?

Cervical spondylomyelopathy (CSM), or wobbler syndrome, is a medical condition that affects the cervical spine. It is characterized by the compression of the spinal cord and/or the nerve roots. This can lead to neurological problems and/or neck pains. Spinal compression can be caused by intervertebral disk slippage and/or skeletal malformation of a narrowed vertebral canal (the bony canal surrounding the soft spinal cord). This disease is called the wobbler syndrome as it describes the characteristically wobbly gait that the affected dog exhibits. It commonly affects large dogs, such as the Great Dane.

Symptoms of wobbler syndrome include:

- abnormal wobbly gait
- neck pain, stiffness
- weakness
- short-stride walking, spastic with a floating appearance or very weak in the front limbs
- possibly unable to walk – partial or complete paralysis
- possible muscle loss near the shoulders
- possible worn or scuffed toenails from uneven walking
- increased extension of all four limbs
- difficulty getting up from lying position

Great Dane Bloat – What Are the Signs Your Dog Is Experiencing This?

Great Danes can suffer from bloat, which is a medical condition which involves the buildup of gas when the stomach is twisted. This can kill your Great Dane within hours if it does not receive immediate medical attention. This can be avoided by feeding your Great Dane small food portions in two to three small meals daily. Never feed your dog extremely large meals, and encourage it to rest for at least one hour, after eating. You should not let your Great Dane have any intense physical activities after its meals. Having a raised food bowl will also help avoid this condition, as it prevents them from having to lay down their legs to eat.

Always observe your Great Dane after eating, and watch out for any signs of an enlarged abdomen, labored breathing, excessive drooling, vomiting, weak pulse, and paleness in the nose and mouth. If you see any of these signs, immediately take your Great Dane to the veterinarian where it will be stabilized, and likely undergo gastric decompression.

Great Dane Vaccinations – Which Should Your Dog Get?

Your Great Dane should have vaccinations to prevent diseases. It can be vaccinated when it has reached eight weeks of age.

Boosters are also essential for puppies so that the antibodies it has acquired from its mother do not interfere with the vaccines' effectiveness. They should receive booster shots approximately at four-week intervals until the puppy is 20 weeks old.

Below are some of the diseases that your Great Dane must get vaccinations for:

- **Canine Distemper.** This is a serious infection and a potentially fatal virus that can impact any dog. But, puppies are more vulnerable. It is easily transmitted from discharges coming from the nose and eyes. It can affect the dog's nervous system. If it survives from this disease, it may have permanent brain damage.

- **Canine Parvo Virus.** This is a resistant virus that can survive in an environment for over 12 months. It is also highly contagious and can affect dogs of all ages. The virus attacks the dog's intestinal lining, where bacteria can enter the blood system. Dogs can die within 24 hours, if not treated immediately.

- **Canine Hepatitis.** It's a highly infectious and fatal disease that can be contracted from another dog's urine. Your dog can suffer from loss of appetite, diarrhea, and abdominal pain. It can also develop long-term kidney and liver problems.

Great Dane Vitamins – Which Should You Give Your Dog?

Nutritional supplements can help your Great Dane have improved health. Consult your veterinarian to determine the best vitamins, dosage, and regimen to give your dog.

Below are some of the supplements you can give your Great Dane:

- **Chondroitin and Glucosamine.** Both help ensure that your Great Dane has stronger joints and aid in repairing damaged joint tissues.
- **Vitamins C and E.** They help maintain collagen levels that help prevent joint tissue damage and inflammation.
- **Fish Oil.** This contains useful anti-inflammatory qualities. When regularly given to your Great Dane, it can help improve its movement and reduce any joint inflammation.
- **MSM (Methyl Sulfonyl Methane).** It can help in maintaining joint tissue condition by enabling your Great Dane's cartilage to absorb water and serve as a cushion for its bones.

Great Dane Weight – How Can You Keep It in a Healthy Range?

It is vital that you do not allow your Great Dane to become overweight. It can be easy for the dog to gain weight, but hard to reduce it. A heavy Great Dane will have a shorter lifespan. The excess weight will cause it as it gets older to have mobility problems.

Maintaining its weight within the healthy range is the easiest way you can extend your Great Dane's life. Here are some ways you can do so:

Your Great Dane should have its vaccinations, to prevent diseases.

- **Provide Small Portion Sizes.** Never feed your Great Dane with one meal that has a large portion above 8 ounces, as this can cause bloat. Instead, divide its meals into small parts throughout the day. Consult your veterinarian for the ideal daily food portion and meal routine for your dog.

- **Daily Exercise.** Allow your Great Dane to walk and run every day, but be careful not to make it too strenuous. Remember to wait at least one hour after its meal before making it do any physical activity.

Great Dane Growth Chart – How Can This Help You?

A growth chart is a way for you to monitor and record your Great Dane's growth. It is a tool for breeders to know if the puppy's growth is healthy, and be alerted to any potential problems. This can make it easy for the breeder to monitor the pups, especially if there are many in the litter. The pup's weight is measured upon its birth and should continue to be done so once or twice weekly.

Owners can also determine the puppies' nutritional requirements with the help of the growth chart. This can aid in detecting any disease or dietary deficiencies. Large breeds like the Great Dane can undergo a growth spurt between birth and four to five months. During this time, a Great Dane pup is expected to gain 2.5 lb. (1.13 kg.) per week, and may vary slightly from week to week. Visit your veterinarian if you do not see any signs that your Great Dane pup is not gaining weight. It could potentially have worms, intestinal upsets, and poor nutrition that can impede its growth.

Below is a sample of a Great Dane growth chart:

Age	Weight (Pounds)	Height (Inches)
At Birth	1 - 2	NA
1 Week	2 - 3	NA
2 Weeks	3 - 5	NA
3 Weeks	4 - 7	NA
4 Weeks	5 - 8	NA
6 Weeks	10 - 20	NA
2 Months	18 - 26	13 - 18
3 Months	30 - 45	17 - 23
4 Months	45 - 65	21 - 26
5 Months	60 - 85	23-30
6 Months	70 - 105	26 - 33
7 Months	75 - 110	27 - 34
8 Months	80 - 120	27 - 35
9 Months	85 - 125	28 - 35
One year	90 - 140	29 - 36
Full-grown	100 - 200	28 - 38

Great Dane Diet and Nutrition – How Can You Maintain Your Dog's Healthy Food Intake?

It is important to establish a consistent feeding schedule and appropriate food portions, especially during the first six months of the puppy's life. Great Danes have various food requirements according to their age, gender, and the amount of exercise they undertake. You may need to feed your puppy three times a day, during the first six months. When it reaches two months old, you may supply it two to four cups of food per day, and increase this amount by one cup every month until the puppy is six months old. By the time the dog is six to nine months of age, you may feed it twice a day. Never feed it at other times of the day, except when giving treats, during training. Remember that your Great Dane's last meal should be approximately two hours before bedtime. Avoid any growth-accelerating formula to prevent any potential joint and bone problems.

CHAPTER 10

Great Dane Care– How Can You Take Care of This Breed?

This chapter discusses the general care a Great Dane needs. When it comes to keeping its physical appearance, this breed is one that is low maintenance. Since it is one of the breeds that has a short coat, you just need to give it a thorough bath 1-2 times per month.

The Great Dane is considered a low maintenance breed, but of course, they can never have too much love!

However, it is important to note that in other areas, such as food and veterinary upkeep, caring for a Great Dane costs much more than the average breed. Some owners allocate hundreds of dollars per month in total maintenance.

The Great Dane is imposing; it is not the type of dog you can just ignore until it behaves or comforts itself.

Great Dane Care – What Do You Need to Know?

You need to understand that the Great Dane has special needs. Issues that involve nutrition, behavior, health, and training are some of the things you need to consider.

Raising A Great Dane – Do You Have What It Takes?

The expenses to care for a small dog, like a Chihuahua, will be hugely different with a Great Dane. For a large (huge) dog, the things you will need to spend will cost triple the amount, on average. You must be prepared to shell out the necessary funds for food and veterinary care.

Some of the expenses you will need to consider include: the initial cost of getting your Great Dane, neutered or spayed, vaccinations, microchipping, essential supplies, pet insurance, worming, and flea treatments. Neutering or spaying procedures can cost $250 or more, while heartworm treatment averages $150 per year.

Veterinary treatments can cost a lot too. Procedures that rectify conditions like bloat can cost up to $6,000. Great Danes are also susceptible to cardiovascular diseases, which can also cost thousands of dollars.

You must also be strong enough to lead the dog, especially during exercise and training. If you or your family do not put in the effort to train and exercise it, the dog will end up becoming stubborn and unsociable. You must be able to muster dominance and assertiveness when giving commands to your dog. Should your Great Dane suddenly pull and run when you are out walking it, you must be able to hold it and not allow yourself to be dragged by the dog.

Great Dane Puppy Care – What Are the Important Things to Remember?

The care you will be giving to a Great Dane puppy will be different from what an adult dog needs. Puppyhood is an exciting time for owners to see how their dog adapts to living with them, training and molding it to become a wonderful member of the family.

Remember to start training your Great Dane puppy early. You can do this on your own or bring it to a dog training school to be handled by professionals. This will be an excellent opportunity for the pup to socialize with other dogs too. Assess the skills and commands your Great Dane will need to learn to live with you.

It will also need regular play and walking sessions. This will give your Great Dane the physical and mental stimulation needed for proper development. Provide your pup with toys that can challenge its mind and body. Remember to let it recharge and rest after a day of play and exercise.

Your puppy will also start teething, so you will need to give it chew toys to spare your furniture and belongings from becoming one! Chew toys will also ensure your pup is gnawing at something that is safe, instead of another object that may injure or affect its health negatively.

Great Dane Running – Is This the Exercise It Needs?

A vital thing to keep in mind when it comes to exercise for your Great Dane is that it must not be excessive and strenuous. Despite its massive frame, Great Danes only need low-level exercise due to their genetic and skeletal build. Running might put too much strain on your Great Dane's legs and joints. To find out the best exercise routine for your Great Dane, consider its age, weight, and health.

Do not allow your Great Dane puppy to undergo any taxing exercises until it turns 18 months of age. Its bones, muscles, joints, and tendons are still developing at this time and might be negatively affected if it does anything that is too vigorous. Because Great Danes are susceptible to joint problems, having them damaged early on will make your dog's life miserable with pain as it grows. A 45 to 60-minute daily walk with your Great Dane should suffice.

Great Dane Shedding – How Can You Manage It?

Great Danes shed as much as other short-haired breeds. You will notice though, that the amount of hair shed is much more compared to smaller dogs. This is solely based on the fact that it has a larger surface area of fur compared to smaller dogs. However, the shedding can become worse if your dog is suffering from skin problems, nutritional, or contact allergies. Another cause of excessive shedding may be low thyroid function.

If you have observed that your Great Dane is shedding more than usual, you may try giving it supplements, such as organic ocean kelp or alfalfa powder. Always consult with your veterinarian if your dog has any skin conditions, and to find the best treatment for the particular condition.

Great Dane Grooming – What Should You Keep in Mind?

Keeping a Great Dane clean and groomed should be a simple task. This breed is easy to maintain in the hygiene department, the only problems you may face are its large size, and its response to bathing. You can bathe and groom it once every three to six weeks. Remember to keep grooming schedules consistent.

Make your Great Dane feel comfortable during baths. You can first observe how it responds to water and soap. If it always tries to escape, a good course of action is to make it feel calm. You can do this by gently brushing the dog, or tire it out a bit by going for a walk, before giving it a bath.

During baths, start by wetting the dog's neck and applying shampoo on its coat and belly. Avoid getting soap and water into the dog's eyes, ears, and nose. Rinse its fur a few times until no traces of cleanser are left. Use towels to dry your dog, and never use a blow dryer. Observe if there are any skin reactions to the soap that you have used on your Great Dane.

Brushing is an excellent opportunity to bond with your Great Dane. With a soft bristle brush or rubber grooming mitt, gently comb through your dog's coat.

You will probably be spending more time caring for your Great Dane's head and face. Wash its face after it ventures outside, or it gets into anything messy. A simple wet washcloth works well.

Check your dog's eyes and ears once every two to three days. Ensure that its eyes are clear and free from infections. The mucus build-up in the eyes causing crust is quite common; just gently wipe the eye corners using a soft cloth to remove. If you observe that there is a continuous watery discharge from the eyes, immediately have the dog examined by the veterinarian. To keep your Great Dane's ears clean, wrap your forefinger with a soft cotton cloth and wipe the dog's ear while massaging the ear canal. You may do this once every week.

To maintain your Great Dane's dental health, look out for any signs of cavities, tartar, and food build-up. Tartar can lead to periodontal disease and cause tooth loss and bacteria to enter the bloodstream. You may opt for a toothbrush or brush that you can slip on your finger, to keep your dog's teeth clean.

Grooming your Great Dane's feet, paws, and nails will help with its movement. Letting the claws grow too long will make standing and walking painful and awkward, as they can curl around your dog's paw. Trim the nails regularly and treat any injuries you can find on your dog's paws.

CHAPTER 11

Great Dane Mixes– What Are the Different Mixed Breeds That Exist?

M ixed-breed Great Danes are a result of mating a pure-bred Great Dane, and another pure-bred dog of another breed. Dogs that are offspring of such a pair are known to be less inclined to inherit genetic disorders. Some of the Great Dane mixes that the American Canine Hybrid Club have recognized are: The Golden Labrador, the Irish Dane, and the Daniff. When buying a mixed-breed Great Dane, make sure you do not purchase them from pet stores, puppy mills, and backyard breeders. The reason is many of these only want to profit by selling trendy mixed-breeds, with little regard for health and living conditions.

*Mixed-breed Great Danes are a result of mating a pure-bred
Great Dane, and another pure-bred dog of another breed.*

Great Dane Mastiff

This mixed-breed is called the Great Daniff, or Daniff, and is recognized by the American Canine Hybrid Club, the International Designer Canine Registry, and the Designer Dogs Kennel Club. This is a huge dog that is affectionate and won't hesitate to protect its family and pack.

Its parent breed is the Great Dane and Mastiff. It can grow into a massive size of 30 to 34 in. (76 to 86 cm.) in height measured from the withers. It can weigh between 115 to 130 lb. (52 to 60 kg.). Its coat is smooth and short and can have the color range of the Great Dane. It combines the elegance of the Great Dane and the muscular build of the Mastiff. It is not too slim nor too bulky. Its legs are long, and the paws are big.

119

Great Dane Rottweiler Mix

This mixed-breed is also known as the Weiler Dane. It can exhibit a variety of colors, including the black and tan markings of the Rottweiler. Its coat is short and sheds moderately.

Unfortunately, this mixed-breed has a short life span, since its parent breeds, the Great Dane, lives an average of 8 years, while the Rottweiler can live up to 11 years. It will be potentially healthier than its parents, but will still be susceptible to medical conditions common in large breeds like hip dysplasia. Both parent breeds are also vulnerable to gastric torsion.

The temperament will still vary for each dog. The genes from the Rottweiler may make the dog's hunting drive stronger.

Great Dane Poodle Mix

This mixed-breed is also known as the Great Danoodle and is a cross between the Great Dane and the Standard Poodle. It has a large physique, a stout body, muscular legs, elongated head and muzzle, round button-like eyes, a dark triangular nose tip, and a long, hanging tail. Great Danoodles will often have a curly coat inherited from its Poodle parent.

It has a gentle and affectionate temperament. They are great with kids and make an excellent member of the family. It is also an intelligent dog and can be trained easily.

Labrador-Great Dane Mix

This mixed-breed is called the Labradane and is a cross between the Great Dane and the Labrador Retriever. It has an average life expectancy of 8 to 12 years. It can weigh between 100 to 180 lb. (45 to 81 kg.) and can stand at 24 to 34 in. (60 to 86 cm.) tall, measured from the withers. It has an athletic stature that is lean and tall. Its coat is short and straight. Its ears are long and floppy and have a long tail that curls. Its eyes can be dark brown or black, and its head is broad. Its coat is straight, short and close to the skin. Common coat colors are white, golden, chocolate, black, blue, cream, and brown.

Dalmatian Great Dane

The Great Dane and Dalmatian are breeds that are known for their loyalty, alertness, and intelligence. Great Danes and Dalmatians may be opposites when it comes to activeness, since the former is more laid back, while the latter is very active. You will need to balance its exercise routine, so it can satisfy its requirements, and at the same time, ensure measures to prevent it from joint problems caused by too much exercise.

Great Dane Hound Mix

Names for this mixed-breed include the Irish Dane and the Great Wolfhound. This is a hybrid of the Great Dane and the Irish Wolfhound. It has an average lifespan of 7 to 10 years. Unlike other designer dogs that have recently emerged, the Great Wolfhound had started to exist in the 1800s when they were bred as an attempt to preserve the Irish Wolfhound.

Its weight can range from 100 to 150 lb. (45 to 68 kg.), and has a height of 32 to 38 in. (81 to 96 cm.) measured from its withers. Its head shape is rectangular, ears that are floppy and drop down, and eyes that are almond-shaped. The fur is straight, and short to medium in length. Common coat colors are black, white, brown, gray, and golden.

German Great Dane

This hybrid dog is called the Great Shepherd and is a product of a pure-bred Great Dane and a German Shepherd. Its average lifespan ranges from 8 to 13 years. It is an excellent mixed-breed to be your family's watchdog. It combines the size and strength of Great Dane and the alertness of the German Shepherd.

This is one of the larger mixed-breeds of the Great Dane. It stands at the height of 28 to 30 in. (71 to 76 cm.), and weigh between 65 to 130 lb. (29 to 58 kg.). It has a long, muscular body and lean legs. The coat color tends to lean towards the Great Dane, with the common ones are black, hazel, merle, and brown.

The Great Shepherd will not be an ideal house companion if you are living in a small space, such as an apartment. It will need a big yard to get plenty of exercise. It requires at least an hour of brisk walking daily.

It will need moderate effort in the grooming department as it typically takes after the Great Dane's coat. It may shed its fur twice in a year and may need to be bathed more regularly than a pure-bred Great Dane. You will need to brush it once a day to keep it healthy and get rid of loose hair.

Great Dane Mix Puppies

Mixed-breed puppies have better genetic diversity. They have a lower chance of inheriting genetic conditions since the mating process naturally leaves out the defective genes. With that said, some of the Great Dane's genetic conditions, such as hip dysplasia and bloat, may be balanced out when bred with another kind of pure-bred dog. However, you will need to find a pure-bred dog that does not share its genetic conditions.

CHAPTER 12

Other Great Dane Information You Need to Know

There may be some more questions you have in mind about Great Danes. For example, is it possible to have a miniature and teacup Great Dane? How about long-haired Great Danes, do they exist? This section will explore the answers to these queries.

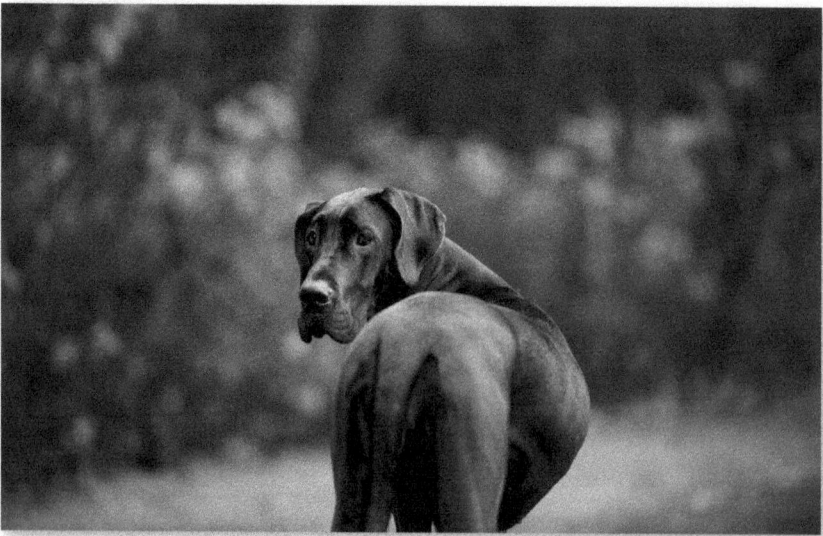

Great Danes are known for their massive size; if you want a smaller dog, then the Great Dane is not for you.

This chapter will also consider how joining a Great Dane dog club can help you become a better owner, and what you need to do to enter. This part will also discuss different dog competitions your Great Dane can enter and excel in.

Miniature Great Danes – What Are Their Characteristics?

A whole lineage of miniature Great Danes simply does not exist. There may be one that is smaller than the rest of its littermates, but it should never be encouraged. This may also be caused by unethical breeding conduct. You will only be subjecting it to health problems, by attempting to breed smaller puppies.

Great Danes are known for their massive size; if you want a smaller dog, then the Great Dane is not for you.

Teacup Great Danes – Do They Exist?

You should be alarmed if you see a person marketing a teacup Great Dane. These smaller-sized dogs are the product of poor breeding and labeled them as such in the hopes of selling them. Great Danes are bred specially for their large size; you just can't manipulate this breed to become smaller. It is also unethical to do so.

Combining a pair to produce a small dog, such as a Chihuahua and a Great Dane, is never recommended because it will naturally not happen due to the drastic difference in size. It will be complicated for the dog to get pregnant, and the puppies would have to be delivered via C-section. You can be sure that these kinds of puppies will have a plethora of health problems.

Long Haired Great Danes – Do They Exist?

Great Danes have naturally short coats. A Great Dane with a long fur is probably a mixed-breed. If you are looking to get a Great Dane with a long coat, your best bet would be to get a Great Danoodle. This mixed-breed will have a longer coat that is slightly curly. Long-haired mixed-breed Great Danes will have a more demanding grooming routine than a pure-bred one. You will need to give it a bath and brush its fur regularly, to keep it clean and healthy.

Great Dane Clubs – What Are the Criteria They Look For?

Great Dane dog clubs organize many events each year to showcase the best dogs in conformation, agility, and obedience. Becoming a member also gives you the chance to meet other Great Dane owners, breeders, and enthusiasts. It will also be a fantastic opportunity for your Great Dane puppy to socialize, where you and the dog can spend quality time in an environment that celebrates the breed.

Becoming a member is simple. Search for a Great Dane dog club in your area online. Note that some of these organizations are not recognized by the AKC. Do sufficient research on what the club's vision, mission, goals, and annual activities are. Once you have found one, explore its website and fill out online application forms for applying to become a member. You will need to pay a membership fee too. For example, the Great Dane Club UK charges £8 annually, for a single membership.

You are required to abide by the club's rules, regulations, and general code of ethics. Some of these laws include ethics on Great Dane breeding, care, and member conduct.

Great Dane Competitions – What Are the Different Kinds and How You Can Enter Your Dog?

There are a number of dog competitions you can have your Great Dane participate in. A committed training routine is required if you want your Great Dane to excel in these contests.

You can train your Great Dane to participate in performance competitions. This usually involves displaying excellence in agility, obedience, tracking, and weight pull.

In agility contests, the dog runs through an obstacle course in a specified time. As the dog and handler improve, they will move up to more challenging levels of competition. Obedience tests are a formal competition, where the dog and the handler work as a team. They start with simple commands, such as heeling and staying. They then progress to challenging retrieval tasks, jumps, and scent article discrimination. Tracking trials test the dog's instinct of smell and have them follow a scent of a specific individual. The dog is judged by its ability to accurately identify and track the smell, under increasingly difficult conditions. Weight pulls are events where the dog's ability to move heavy weights are tested.

CHAPTER 13

Conclusion

There is no doubt that the Great Dane can be the perfect addition to your family. It is an affectionate dog with a mild temper, which can make it an excellent companion for your kids. It is fondly known as a "gentle giant"; behind its imposing physique is a dog who would choose to lounge on the couch and snuggle with you, though it's important to set boundaries with your dog.

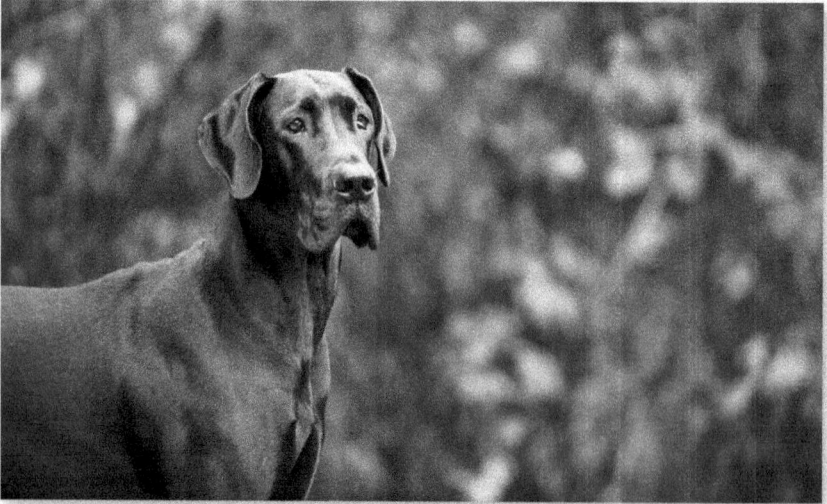

It takes serious responsibility, commitment, and dedication to own and care for a Great Dane.

Images of dogs resembling the Great Dane have been around for thousands of years. Because of their strength, size, and agility, they were chosen as partners in hunting. In Europe, they were especially used for hunting wild boars. They also became companions to noblemen and lived luxurious lives. The Great Dane even became the national dog of Germany in the 18th century, and around the same time, they started to arrive in the United States.

If you plan on buying a Great Dane, be sure to get one from a responsible and reputable breeder. Never buy one from backyard breeders and pet stores, who probably produce their dogs in puppy mills. Responsible breeders will ensure their dogs are checked and are safe from genetic conditions and only aim to improve the breed's gene pool. Do some diligent research where responsible breeders can be found, and be prepared to ask him or her questions that will ensure that the dog you are getting is healthy.

The Great Dane's average lifespan is only seven to eight years, which is shorter than the average dog's. It is susceptible to a number of health conditions. Among these are bloat, wobbler syndrome, and hip dysplasia. These can be fatal to your Great Dane if it does not receive any immediate medical attention. Regular veterinary check-ups will keep your Great Dane in top shape.

You need to understand that caring for a Great Dane will demand higher expenses for food, toys, and other supplies. A dog bed, crate, kennel, leash, and collar are some of the essential items you must provide. Since these will be bigger in size, be prepared to pay more. Remember to check your Great Dane's size to get items that will best fit your dog.

It takes serious responsibility, commitment, and dedication to own and care for a Great Dane. This dog has unique needs when it comes to training, grooming, and feeding, which you will need to apply to keep it healthy throughout its life. The knowledge you have acquired from this book will help you respond to its needs and help you have a fantastic relationship with your Great Dane. Enjoy the journey!

Your Trusted Great Dane Resource List

This resource list will give you details on breeder and rescue shelter locations, and further information on the Great Dane breed. This guide will provide you with a jumpstart on researching sources where you can get your Great Dane.

Great Dane Breeders in the USA

- **Neet Great Danes**
  http://www.neetdanes.com,
  based in Southern California

- **Wolfpack Great Danes**
  http://wolfpackgreatdanes.com,
  based in Anchorage, Alaska

- **TDT Great Danes & Beagles**
  http://www.tdtgreatdanes.net/,
  based in Interior Alaska

- **Enzodane Great Danes and Ibizans**
  http://enzodane.com,
  based in Arizona

- **Azulene Great Danes**
  http://www.azulenedanes.com/,
  based in Northern California

- **Bent-On Danes**
  http://bent-ondanes.com/,
  based in Southern California

- **Davishire Danes**
  http://davishiredanes.com/,
  based in Sacramento

- **Ink Spots Great Danes**
  http://inkspotsgreatdanes.com/,
  based in Inland Empire

- **JGD Great Danes**
  http://jgdgreatdanes.yolasite.com/

- **KC Danes**
  http://www.kcdanes.com/,
  based in Fremont, California

- **LA Danes**
  http://ladanes.com,
  based in San Clemente, California

- **Paxton Great Danes**
  http://paxtondanes.com/,
  based in Napa Valley, California

- **PCH Danes**
  http://www.pchdanes.com/,
  based in Southern California

- **Sum-Dane Great Danes**
  http://www.sum-danegreatdanes.com/,
  based in Central Valley, California

- **Glacier Danes**
  http://www.glacierdanes.net/,
  based in Parker Colorado

- **Ocean Blue Danes**
  http://www.oceanbluedanes.com/,
  based in Palm Beach County, Florida
- **Fendane Great Danes**
  http://www.fendanegreatdanes.com/,
  based in North Fort Myers, Florida
- **McEmm Great Danes**
  http://mcemn.com/,
  based in Valrico, Florida
- **Caeruleus Great Danes**
  http://caeruleusdanes.com/,
  based in Marietta, Georgia
- **EIO Danes**
  http://eiodanes.com/,
  based in Waterloo, Illinois
- **Foto Danes**
  http://www.fotodanes.com/,
  based in Newton, Iowa
- **Davis Dane**
  http://www.davis-dane.com/,
  based in Hanover, Massachusetts
- **Creek Danes**
  http://www.creekdanes.com/,
  based in Boyne City, Michigan
- **Old Mission Danes**
  http://www.oldmissiondanes.com/,
  based in Imlay City, Michigan

- **Danemark Danes**
  http://danemarkdanes.com/,
  based in St. Charles, Missouri
- **Liberty Danes**
  http://libertydanes.com/dogs.html,
  based in Troy, Missouri
- **Unity Great Danes**
  http://www.unitygreatdanes.com/,
  based in Cleveland, Ohio
- **DaVinci Danes**
  http://davincidanes.wixsite.com/home,
  based in Rockwood, Tennessee
- **Von Bonehenge Great Danes**
  http://vonbonehenge.com/,
  based in El Paso, Texas
- **Ellenni Danes**
  http://www.ellennidanes.com/,
  based in Bealeton, Virginia
- **Daynakin Great Danes LLC**
  http://daynakingreatdanes.com/,
  based in Ferndale, Washington
- **Laurado Great Danes, Registered**
  http://lauradogreatdanes.com/,
  based in Coleville, Washington

Great Dane Breeders in Canada

- **Great Dane Club of Canada breeder directory**
  http://greatdaneclubofcanada.ca/find-a-breeder/

- **Dantry Danes**
  http://dantry.ca/,
  based in Ontario, Canada
- **Jonnie Danes**
  http://www.jonniedanes.com/
- **Strider Great Danes**
  https://www.striderdanes.ca/,
  based in Selkirk, Canada
- **Bosworth Danes**
  http://www.bosworthdanes.com/,
  based in Southern Ontario, Canada
- **Dames Saving Danes Rescue**
  http://damessavingdanes.ca/,
  based in Eastern Ontario, Canada

Great Dane Breeders in the UK

- **Kennel Club (UK) Assured Breeders directory**
  https://www.thekennelclub.org.uk/services/public/acbr/
  Default.aspx?breed=Great+Dane
- **Ravendane Great Danes**
  http://www.ravendane.com/,
  based in Cheshire, England
- **Dainoak Great Danes**
  https://www.dainoakgreatdanes.com/meet-our-danes
- **Dainwood Great Danes**
  http://www.dainwood.co.uk/,
  based in Nottinghamshire, England

Great Dane Rescue Shelters in the USA

- **Harlequin Haven Great Dane Rescue**
  http://hhdane.com/,
  based in Bethel, Ohio
- **Great Dane Rescue of North Texas**
  https://www.danerescue.net/frequently-asked-questions,
  based in Carrolton, Texas
- **Alachua County Humane Society**
  http://www.alachuahumane.org/,
  based Gainesville, Florida
- **Maumelle Friends of the Animals**
  http://maumellefoa.org/,
  based in Maumelle, Arkansas
- **Great Dane Rescue**
  http://www.greatdanerescueinc.com/,
  based in Plymouth, Michigan
- **Seattle Purebred Dog Rescue (SPDR)**
  http://www.spdrdogs.org/,
  based in Redmond, Washington
- **Northwest Great Dane Rescue**
  http://www.northwestgreatdanerescue.com,
  based in Deer Park, Washington
- **Alternative Humane Society**
  https://www.alternativehumanesociety.com/,
  based in Bellingham, Washington
- **Valhalla Rescue**
  http://www.valhallarescue.org/,
  based in Winlock, Washington

Great Dane Club of America & Affiliated Clubs and Rescues

- **Great Dane Club of America**
  http://www.gdca.org,
  based in Kemblesville, Pennsylvania
- **Great Dane Club of Tucson**
  https://www.gdct.org/
- **Indian Dane Rescue**
  http://www.indiandanerescue.com/
- **Great Dane Rescue of Northern California**
  http://gdrnc.org/
- **Rocky Mountain Great Dane Rescue, Inc.**
  http://rmgreatdane.org/,
  based in Aurora, Colorado but also serves Kansas, Nebraska, Utah, Wyoming, Idaho, Montana, New Mexico, Arizona, Oklahoma, Iowa, Missouri and South Dakota
- **Great Dane Club of Greater Denver, Inc. (referrals only).**
  Contact person: Gisela Bussy LeFor and Barbara Grote, contact number: 303-688-8692, 303-699-7037
- **Mid-Atlantic Great Dane Rescue League, Inc.**
  http://www.padanerescue.com/
- **Great Dane Rescue of South Florida,**
  based in Jupiter, Florida. Contact person: Anna Smith, contact number 561-748-4017
- **Great Dane Rescue of Tampa Bay, Inc.**
  http://www.greatdanerescueoftampabay.com/,
  based in Tampa, Florida

- **Great Dane Love - A Central Florida Rescue, Inc.**
  http://www.gdlcf.org/,
  based in Cocoa, Florida
- **Great Dane Club of North Central Florida**
  http://www.gdcncf.org/
- **Bayou Great Dane Rescue**
  http://bayoudane.com/,
  based in Southwest Louisiana
- **The Mid-Atlantic Great Dane Rescue League, Inc.**
  http://www.magdrl.org/

Great Dane Rescue Shelters in Canada

- **Great Dane Angels**
  https://www.greatdaneangels.org/,
  based in Ontario, Canada
- **Danes in Distress**
  http://www.danesindistress.com/
- **For the Love of Danes**
  http://loveofdanesrescue.org/,
  based in Alberta, Canada
- **New Hope for Danes Great Dane Rescue**
  http://www.newhopefordanes.org/,
  based Manitoba and Saskatchewan, Canada

Great Dane Rescue Shelters in the UK

- **The Kennel Club UK directory for Great Dane adoption and rescue shelters**
  https://www.thekennelclub.org.uk/services/public/
  findarescue/Default.aspx?breed=5124

- **Great Dane Adoption Society**
  http://www.danes.org.uk/,
  based in Lincolnshire, England

- **National Great Dane Rescue**
  http://www.ngdr.co.uk/,
  based in Wiltshire, England

- **Daneline International Charitable Foundation**
  https://www.daneline.co.uk,
  based in Bristol, England

- **T J Danes Rescue**
  http://tjdanesrescues.org.uk

www.ingramcontent.com/pod-product-compliance
Lightning Source LLC
Chambersburg PA
CBHW072155090426
42740CB00012B/2280